Team Leadership

Team Leadership

Charles J. Margerison

THOMSON

Australia • Canada • Mexico • Singapore • Spain • United Kingdom • United States

Team Leadership

Copyright © Charles J. Margerison 2002

The Thomson logo is a registered trademark used herein under licence.

For more information, contact Thomson, High Holborn House, 50-51 Bedford Row, London, WC1R 4LR or visit us on the World Wide Web at: http://www.thomsonlearning.co.uk

British Library Cataloguing-in-Publication Data
A catalogue record for this book is available from the British Library

ISBN 1-86152-863-9

First edition published 2002 by Thomson
Reprinted by Thomson in 2002

Typeset by Dexter Haven Associates, London
Printed in the UK by TJ International, Padstow, Cornwall

Contents

List of figures

Preface

There are times when we see the world differently. Galileo Galilei helped us all march forward by proposing that the earth was not the centre of the universe, although he was decried at the time as a heretic. James Watt watched steam boiling away into thin air. He changed the world when he proposed capturing and using it. Today, we live in an age in which it seems whatever we think of is possible, thanks particularly to the magic of telecommunications and the Internet. Ideas now move quicker between one person and another.

However, any innovation depends primarily upon top-class leadership and teamwork to move it forward. This book provides a leadership and team system that anyone can use. It is based on nine major skills necessary in every business and team. These can improve your work contribution. They also give guidance on how to make the best use of your time. In so doing, you can work more effectively with your team. Reciprocally, if they understand the system, they can work more effectively with you.

The key to the system is the Team Wheel. At the centre of this wheel is a term called 'Linking'. It is often said that the strength of a chain is dependent on its weakest link. Likewise, in a company, success depends on how effective the members are at Linking, both internally and externally, to achieve the objectives.

This book shows how to improve your team leadership Linking skills in projects and teams. It also provides a focus for developing your career. Linking skills, plus the eight major work functions, will transform the way you look at your job, at your team and the work that you do.

The concept of the Team Wheel emerged when I was working with major oil companies, such as Shell, Mobil, Burmah Castrol and BP, on team projects. It was later extended to teamwork in banks, telecommunications, hospitals, publishing organizations, computer companies and other organizations with Dr Dick McCann, who had special expertise in computing and statistics. We took the original ideas and jointly developed the work into Team Management Systems (TMS), with a range of feedback products and services. These are now used in over 40 countries. We also developed the Institute of Team Management Studies, through which we have researched in depth the issues covered in this book.

This work also reflects the learning gained from many of my consulting applications with large companies. I have applied the Team Wheel and TMS to a range of commercial problems and opportunities, and some of these cases are included in this book, with due confidentiality. In these cases, I specifically focus on personal team leadership skills. They are at the heart of the team management. Where possible, I have quoted the real names of those involved in the cases and examples, but in some cases this has not been possible, in order to ensure confidentiality.

The Team Wheel has two aspects. One deals with work tasks, the other with personal preferences. In the first half of the book, I will focus more on the work tasks, and in the second half on the personal work preferences aspect.

As you read the book, it is useful to be proactive and see how you can apply the key points in your job. It is useful to ask how effective you are at Linking, both internally and externally, on the key work functions of the Team Wheel. You will improve your overall work performance, many times over, just by putting your energy, and effort, into understanding these and applying them.

It has taken two years to write this book, and various people have helped in many ways. Nikki Mead's work at our Institute of Team Management Studies is reflected in the data presented in the final chapter. Thanks also to Dr Dick McCann for his work with TMS over the years, and for the contribution to the text based on our internal documents and other publications. Thanks also to Barry Smith for his careful reading of the draft and practical suggestions. Also, thanks to Dr Jim Kable for his long-standing advice on various issues. Appreciation also to Anna Faherty for her faith in the work and facilitating the publication.

As always, my main thanks go to my wife, Colinette. She is a team manager and Linker par excellence.

Charles J. Margerison
January 2002

Introduction

This book puts forward a new approach to leadership based on the Margerison McCann Team Management Wheel. This is a practical tool derived from work with major companies, such as Shell Oil, Hewlett Packard, Sony, ICI, Mobil, and government organizations in more than 40 countries.

By reading this book and applying the Team Management System (or TMS), you will see within a short time many personal and business benefits. The book provides clear guidance on how to:

- assess leadership strengths
- develop effective teamwork
- improve problem-solving
- provide Linking and co-ordination skills across the team
- achieve more in less time
- improve both individual and team performance.

Every job can be improved with a tried and tested system. This book is based on the work of managers and their teams. The benefits of the approach are:

- You will gain a system that works.
- The system is well researched, with over 750,000 leaders and team members involved.
- It is based on the Team Wheel, in which nine key areas for effective action are presented.
- The Team Wheel is a master tool that can be used daily to manage tasks, time and relationships.
- At the centre of the system is the practice of Linking, and mastery of this is the key to effective leadership.
- You can improve your personal effectiveness by understanding your team work preferences, and those of other team members.

- The Team Wheel can be used to plan your career development.
- Using the system will lead to better business links, both internally and externally.
- Real results will be achieved by applying the system, from reducing costs to improving sales.
- Leadership skills can be gained by learning the language of teamwork based on TMS.

CHAPTER ONE

Nine key Team Leadership skills – focus points for action

A system for teamwork

In your work you are usually involved in at least one team, and also various teamwork projects. Some of the team projects may be part of a regular team. Others will be temporary assignments to solve problems or to chase opportunities. We are increasingly assessed by our team contribution.

Knowing how to contribute effectively, either as a member or leader, is a key to success. This is not always easy as teams may not perform as they should. The individuals may be technically competent, but as members of a team they find it difficult to work together. This is the starting-point for thinking about team systems and team management when working with a large petrochemical organization.

CASE STUDY

I was invited by Shell Oil to assist in the development of their refinery work teams. The senior managers were concerned about the standard of work, and that many of the project teams were not delivering on time. The people in the teams were technically qualified. However, the teams were underperforming because they did not work well together.

Prior to my involvement, the company had given team members a high standard of normal training. They invested in the skills development of their staff, and assumed that this individual-based training would lead to better teamwork on such issues as safety, cost control, technology maintenance and problem-solving. Lectures, cases studies, role plays, training films and special exercises had all been tried. The performance levels of the teams had not shown significant improvement.

In the review meeting, the question was asked, 'What else can be done?' One member said, 'Let's lock them up in a room until they agree on how they will work together'. Initially, this remark was taken with some amusement, but it became the key idea for action. I was asked, together with another consultant, to take 20 managers, mainly engineers, to an off-site conference centre in North Wales for two days. We each consulted with a group of 10 people, and I started my meeting by saying:

> I am Charles Margerison. I have been asked by the company to conduct this workshop. Unlike other courses you may have attended, there are no lectures, no written cases or role plays, and no pre-set course agenda. We have two days to discuss any work issues that you think can help improve teamwork. We have a white-board, and I will write up any issues you would like to discuss.

There was a silence in the room. The managers found it hard to believe what I had said. They had been taken away from work, where they were all very busy, to an off-site resort, at great cost to the company. They had assumed it would be a course like many others that they had attended. But this time there was no course and no agenda. One of the managers asked me to clarify the situation. I recounted what had been discussed at the planning meeting. I said that we had two days to discuss any matters that they felt would be helpful in their work as leaders and, in particular, teamwork issues.

After a couple of minutes, during which I asked them to think of issues that were important to them, one manager said he would like to discuss industrial relations agreements and the management of staff. He explained that they were the cause of many team problems. Another engineer said, 'It would be useful to discuss motivation', as he felt that as a manager, that he did not know enough about the subject.

One manager said he had recently been appointed and that he would 'welcome advice on how to work with his new team'. Soon we had a good list of important topics, and conversations to match. The two days flew by. At the end of the workshop, everyone said that they had gained a lot, but they had also contributed just as much by helping each other think through their issues.

On my way home, I reflected that we had made progress, but noted some important points. The discussions had helped managers think through their plans and increased their confidence. However, they indicated that it would be helpful to have a system that helped them to understand how teams worked. They also had mentioned their own personal leadership issues and the need for a process that could be helpful.

In particular I also noted that the members did not have a common teamwork language. They all spoke English, and most had a common engineering language on the technical issues. However, they did not have a common language to deal with team issues.

Team Management Systems

Subsequently the company asked me to follow up the managers, and to meet them in their place of work. At these meetings I discussed what they intended to do to improve teamwork and how they planned to do it. It was in these meetings that the original idea for TMS, and the language of teamwork began to take shape, though it took a number of years to develop a well-tested system.

From my discussions, I knew that the 'language' had to be straightforward and not academic in tone. It had to reflect the language that was used every day at work. It had to be built into a system that everyone could understand. This book outlines TMS, and the language that has now been used by well over a million people in their work.

The good news is that both at the personal level and the team level, these problems are more easily resolved once you have a system. Our work with organizations in industry, commerce and government is based on nine key work factors that are essential in every project and every team.

Throughout our work with project teams in Europe, North America, Southeast Asia and Australasia, we have found that these nine factors assist managers and their teams work together more effectively. The cases in this book outline what we have done to help team leaders and team members solve their process issues.

Teamwork language

Communication starts with a shared language. If you are visiting a foreign country it is useful to be able to understand and communicate in that language. The same is true in teamwork, as there are different technical languages within and between teams.

Team projects often do not work effectively because of communication problems. Increasingly, project groups are made up of team members from different professions. They speak different technical languages. They will have different styles or work preferences. They need a common understanding of a system in order to succeed, particularly as deadlines get closer, and costs rise.

In the Shell case mentioned above the managers had a clear idea of what they did in their own areas. The refinery people said they produced the oil. The accountants said they gave good advice. The research people said they innovated. The sales people said they promoted the products. The safety people said they inspected and maintained operations. They all had a focus. But they did not all share the same focus or understand each other's priorities.

To help reduce the communication problems we therefore developed a language of teamwork. This shared language cuts through misunderstanding and barriers, and speeds up action. It can help both established teams and temporary project teams.

The cross-functional, or process team, which sometimes has a life of only a few months, is a feature of most organizations today. Such teams need to perform effectively right from the start of the project. This is where a shared language of teamwork is also vital.

Key team performance factors

Nine key teamwork factors emerged through discussions with people in different industries. These cover all aspects of teamwork in every organization. The team system work factors are listed below, with a short definition for each.

There are eight distinct work functions, and one all-encompassing area of co-ordination work called Linking. The eight work functions are integrated, using the important concept of Linking:

- Advising: gathering and reporting information.
- Innovating: creating and experimenting with ideas.
- Promoting: exploring and presenting opportunities.
- Developing: assessing and planning applications.
- Organizing: organizing staff and resources.
- Producing: concluding and delivering outputs.
- Inspecting: controlling and auditing contracts and procedures.
- Maintaining: upholding and safeguarding standards and values.
- Linking: co-ordinating and integrating the work of others.

The TMS, which is based on the above factors has been used in over 40 countries and diverse cultures, including:

- North and South America
- Europe
- Arabia
- Africa
- Southeast Asia
- Australasia
- China.

In particular it has been used in economically developed countries such as France, Germany, Singapore, Australia, the UK and US and in countries with substantially different cultures, such as Malaysia, Saudi Arabia, Papua New Guinea and Fiji.

We have researched teams in different types of industries, to find out what makes the difference between high- and low-performing teams. We found that it is vital for any team to cover the nine key factors as the basis of outstanding teamwork. As a result the system has been used by commercial organizations, government agencies, voluntary organizations and community groups. It has even been used by military mountaineering teams climbing Everest and other peaks to help improve their teamwork.

The Team Management Wheel

The nine factors are arranged in a model known as the Margerison McCann Team Management Types of Work Wheel shown in Figure 1.1. For ease of use I shall refer to this as the Team Wheel. Research has shown that the eight outer factors (known as the types of work functions) describe the fundamental different work activities, whereas the central activity of Linking is common to all work functions.

To realize the full potential of teamwork, all teams must perform well on all of the nine factors. In other words, the team needs to be able to self-correct. The Team Wheel is the key visual. Teams in many countries and companies have found it to be invaluable as an *aide memoire* to guide their thinking and effort.

There are two aspects to the Team Wheel. The one shown in Figure 1.1 relates to team tasks and functions. The other one, described later, focusses on the personal aspects and work preferences.

FIGURE 1.1: The Margerison McCann Team Wheel

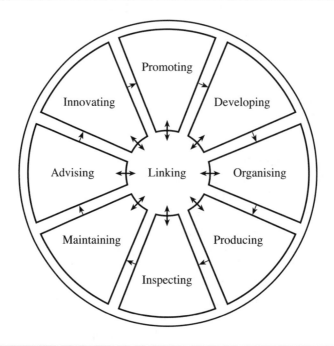

Benefits of the team language system

To self-diagnose and self-correct, it is important to have a model of work based on real-life activity. It provides a checklist for action. The Team Wheel is therefore a practical tool. It has some important characteristics:

- It provides a framework to assess the strengths and weaknesses of a team.
- Each member can assess their own personal strengths using the system, and a fully validated questionnaire has been developed for this purpose.
- The Team Wheel shows the areas that need to be linked together to obtain integrated rather than partial action.
- It provides a system to help relationships between two or more teams to link and co-ordinate their work.
- It is based on the language used every day in the factory, the office, the laboratory or wherever work takes place.
- For individuals, the language and the visual model provide an easy-to-use system for discussing their job, their priorities and contribution to teamwork.

- It is also a valuable tool for individuals to assess their career plans and development.
- It can help make choices to move into new work, or deliberately take a job to widen your experience.

All team members need to understand the nine key factors and to be able to diagnose when things start to go wrong. If any factor is weak the team needs to analyze its deficiencies and take corrective action. Similarly, the Team Wheel provides the same opportunity for an individual team member to assess their contribution, their training needs, their career direction and the way they work.

CASE STUDIES

The Team Wheel has provided the basis for a number of organizations to assess their strengths and weaknesses. Here are some short examples:

- A publishing company concluded it was strong on Innovating, Promoting, and Developing, but had to improve their Producing, where they frequently missed deadlines, and Inspecting, where too many editing errors occurred.
- A manufacturing organization that felt it was strong on Producing and Maintaining, but weak on Promoting and Innovating.
- A company of architects realized it was strong on Innovating and Inspecting, but not as strong on Organizing, and weak on Promoting.
- A bank that felt it was strong on Advising, Inspecting, Producing and Organizing, but they needed to improve its Innovating and Promoting.

Linking is the main force

At a personal level, the same analysis applies. Each person has strengths around the Team Wheel, and other areas which are not as strong. This is normal, and to be expected. This is the main reason for having a team, so that each person can complement the other with their respective strengths. However, this can only happen if there are good links between the team members.

The old saying that 'a chain is only as strong as its weakest link' is true. So it is in any team or organization. You can have, for example, some people Innovating brilliantly, but unless they have good links with those that will be Developing the product and service, their efforts will go nowhere. Likewise, you can have people who are Producing effectively, but unless they are linked closely with those who are Promoting the product or service then poor results are likely.

We developed the term 'Linking' after watching many teams, and many managers and team members. We found their skills of linking both people and things were the main factor that determined success in their overall team-management contribution.

Linking involves co-ordinating and integrating. We chose Linking because it captures a wide range of skills and abilities required by all team members. It reflects the strength required to hold people together. In this book, I will show what effective Linking is, and how to do it. Linking is a set of skills which can be learned, regardless of whether your main work function is Innovating, Organizing, Maintaining or Producing.

CASE STUDY

One of my clients worked for a large company as their Chief Chemist. He was promoted to Technical Director. As a result, he had many specialists reporting to him. He acknowledged that he had little idea of what they did in detail. He concluded that his main role was to act as a Linker, and to get them working closer together.

This insight enabled him to develop a successful relationship with team members. He held a team meeting and indicated what he meant by the term Linking. They had a discussion on how they felt the team should be managed. By having a common language and system, the team members were better able to work together.

What is your Team Management contribution?

Your contribution is the most important thing that you can give to a team. You will be selected to do a job because you have experience, skills and qualifications. However, none of these are worth much unless you contribute to the total team effort. That requires an understanding and application of the nine aspects in the Team Wheel.

It is useful to ask team members what each person feels they can best contribute to the total team effort? You will hear people mention the nine factors in the Team Wheel, albeit in different words, such as dealing with details, coming up with ideas, providing good information or working to a system and delivering on time. These are crucial factors in any team.

Look at your team contribution. In how many of the areas of the Team Wheel do you add value to the team? Some members contribute in all the nine major areas. Some confine their contribution to one or two areas. However, if you are involved in a leadership role you need to learn how to contribute in all the main areas.

How to assess team members' contribution

Anyone who is managing a team or leading a project is managing a small organization. All the functions that take place in a large organization take place in a team or project. Using the Team Wheel you can check how well each of the main areas link together, and how well the individual members link together. The following questions provide important indicators:

- Advising: how well do your team members provide advice to each other and people outside the team?
- Innovating: to what extent do your team members just do the job as laid down or do they look for ways of making improvements by Innovating?
- Promoting: all teams have to promote what they do and influence others. How well does your team do this?
- Developing: ensuring that systems and products are well developed takes time, and requires considerable Linking skills internally and externally. How do you rate your team and each of the members on this?
- Organizing: implementing any plan requires organization and a systematic approach. How well does your team do this?
- Producing: nothing is finally achieved until something is produced. This requires a lot of internal team Linking, but also external Linking with suppliers. How well does your team perform?
- Inspecting: this is not always the most popular of activities, but it is essential for high-quality work. How effective is your team, not only at doing the Inspecting work, but Linking with others to ensure they gain support?
- Maintaining: all operations require both physical and personal maintenance. It is a function that depends on strong links with others' activities. How well do you and your team perform in this area?

Let us look at a couple of real examples of what poor leadership Linking can mean. On the surface you may say the problems were obvious. They were, but only after the event. However, with good leadership Linking the problems could have been avoided.

CASE STUDY: SALES AND MANUFACTURING LINKS

A textile company, which I consulted, developed a profitable business in the sale of a new range of ties for social occasions. As a result, it increased the production order and built a considerable stock. In fact, it over-anticipated the growth of the business and put far more into stock than was immediately required. Then the orders started to drop very quickly, but production continued.

In the subsequent review of why the company lost money, a number of points emerged which relate directly to the lack of teamwork. The manufacturing department had spare capacity and decided, without consulting the sales team, to increase production. Secondly, the sales team, when it realized that sales were declining, decided to double its efforts and did not have a meeting with the manufacturing team. With hindsight, everyone could see that there had been poor communication and that the links were not in place to prevent a considerable loss.

In this case, the people promoting the product were more interested in getting out to sell than in talking to their internal colleagues. Also, the people involved in Producing decided to increase output without Linking with those who were Promoting. It was decided in the review that everyone involved should spend more time on their Advising and Inspecting work, and various systems were put in place, only somewhat late.

CASE STUDY: MAKING TEAM SYSTEMS WORK

Another example, recently published in the newspapers, concerns a national airline. It was reported that six of its fleet of Boeing 767 jet airliners had to be withdrawn from service, all at once, because they had not been serviced at the due date. As a result, services were cancelled and a public outcry was raised. Some of these planes were six months overdue on their service. Clearly safety standards had been violated and the public put at risk.

Of course excuses were paraded as reasons. However, it was a clear issue of teamwork breaking down. The Organizing and Producing – 'keep the planes flying' messages were taking precedence over the Inspecting and Maintaining functions. Team leaders in this case were badly adrift in their priorities.

It is one thing to have a system to diagnose problems. It is another thing to come forward with solutions. This book will provide examples of how the Team Wheel and the nine major work areas can make a practical difference. We shall look specifically at each of the work functions, and indicate action that can be taken at the personal, the team and the organizational levels.

Summary

We talk about things going well by using terms like, 'as smooth as clockwork', or going like a 'well-oiled machine'. We like to see such activity when we go to a restaurant, or turn up at a hotel, or board a train or plane. If the service breaks down, we expect someone to diagnose the problem quickly, and to find a solution.

That activity in itself involves a review of why the link in the chain has broken down. It requires someone to be effective at leadership Linking. It means being effective in getting people to ask questions, and then to concentrate on all areas of the Team Wheel. It is when a crisis occurs that you can usually see how effective team members are at teamwork and Linking.

- Do they know how to find the right information?
- Do they know who to bring in for assistance?
- Do they link the people and the systems to get effective action?

In the following chapters, we will examine each of the key factors of the Margerison McCann Team Wheel in turn, and look at ways various teams which have used them to improve team performance.

EXERCISE

1. What are the main strengths of your team on the Team Wheel categories?
2. Where do you need to put most effort to gain improvements?

CHAPTER TWO

Team applications – practical ways and means

In this chapter you can get to grips with the use of the Team Wheel by reviewing some case examples and applications. All of the cases are based on personal experiences, including those that occurred before the development of the Team Wheel, but can now be understood in the context of the system

It is unusual for a team to put equal effort into all areas of the Team Wheel at the same time. Each day, teams as well as individuals allocate time and effort towards two main things:

■ dealing with problem and opportunity situations as they arise
■ meeting the personal preferences and needs of the team members.

The following applications and examples indicate the way the Team Wheel can be used as the basis for team and personal development.

Promoting and Producing

While working on an assignment for a major US bank, I noticed that the sales and technical staff did not communicate well. Although they rarely met, they were antagonistic to each other. The aim of the sales force was to persuade corporate customers to buy into a new electronic approach to banking. The sales people Promoting the new services often 'oversold', not realizing some of the technical issues of delivery. When the technical people came to install the system, they often found the specifications that they were given did not match the real needs, or could not be produced on time.

After a number of expensive mistakes, the bank decided on a new team approach. Instead of sales people working separately, concentrating on Promoting, and the technical people following in afterwards on the Producing and delivery aspects, they agreed to establish a team of two (one sales person and one technical person) for each assignment.

Under the new system, whenever a specification had to be made a technical specialist accompanied the sales person on his or her visit to the client. This of course raised the cost, but over time was found to be a more successful and economical way of doing the job. Focussing on both Promoting and the technical aspects of Producing during each meeting covered two parts of the Team Wheel. When it came to product delivery, clients got what they wanted, without costly delays or mistakes. The major problems of communication were overcome by joint working. It sounds simple after the event, but it took a long time to get the right approach.

CASE STUDY: SOCIAL SERVICES

A social services team was formed to ensure that homeless families were provided with proper care. A homeless families centre was established in a large suburban house for mothers and children, while fathers were expected to find lodgings and seek a new home for the family.

Early in my career I worked in this team, and learned a lot about questioning assumptions and management as a result of the experience.

When I joined the social services team, the homeless families unit was always full and there was a waiting list. The social services team felt that they were doing a good job by finding homeless families and providing a place to care for them. They defined their role as primarily that of Maintaining and Advising. By providing care, they were trying to maintain the family as a unit and at the same time give advice on how they could find permanent accommodation.

Rob Baker, a new manager, was appointed as leader of our team. He felt the costs were too high, so he set an objective to solve the homeless problem and close the homeless units.

At a meeting with the social services team, he said,

Most people become homeless because they can't, or won't, pay their rent. So, it is up to our team to help families pay their rent in the first instance.

Some team members objected, saying that their job was to help counsel families in need, not be rent collectors. Baker said,

If we solve the homeless problem, we can use our counselling skills on other cases.

As a result of this redefinition of our work priorities, the team members telephoned every major landlord in the city. We asked them to indicate those families that were in danger of eviction. Baker then allocated the names and addresses of these families to the team members. We were asked to visit the families on the day they received their pay or social security money. The task was to obtain the rent as the first payment before a family spent it on food, drink, gambling or other activities.

Baker changed the priorities of the team from Advising and Maintaining to Inspecting and Linking with the landlords and families. The results were dramatic. Within one year, there were no homeless families applying for accommodation. This resulted in the closure of the homeless families unit.

Instead of Maintaining the families at great cost, the social services team solved the problem by collecting and paying their rent. In team management terms, they changed their allocation of effort, and as a result solved a problem.

CASE STUDY: PROJECT MANAGEMENT

The success of any project depends on how quickly the people can form an effective team. The team selected may have all the technical skills. However, many projects fail to deliver on time to the required level because they do not understand how to make a temporary team work. I have been involved with many project teams.

The Team Wheel has proved to be an effective way of focussing on the issues to improve project management. This has been done directly using the Wheel as a visual aid, and with feedback profiles that are based on self-assessments by team members. They then share these profiles as a basis for discussion and planning.

That is how my colleagues and I helped a chemical company bring together various project teams to work on safety and security issues. Until this time, the main focus was placed on the Inspecting function. Once they understood the Team Wheel, they realized they needed a plan for all areas and, in particular the Advising, Promoting and Linking work that was required.

CASE STUDY: INNOVATING AND ORGANIZING

In another consulting assignment, with a policy advisors' group in a government department, I noted that major work preferences were in the Advising and Innovating areas. Problems arose, however, when staff were asked to take on more administrative work and team leadership roles. Many of them felt that was not a major part of their job, and something to be avoided.

I introduced them to the Team Wheel, and we discussed its application to their work.

This led to a discussion about the changes the members would need to make in order to become effective in the Organizing area. After this discussion the policy advisers recognized that taking on a new role did not mean giving up their Innovating and Advising work. Instead, it meant adding the Organizing aspect to their job. As a result, we were able to assist them in designing training programmes on a range of activities. These included the practical aspects of organizing and managing projects, together with the selection and recruitment of staff, conducting meetings and establishing budgets.

CASE STUDY: INSPECTING AND MAINTAINING

A professional society with a large membership conducted a review of its work. The result showed that it had a limited view of its role within the eight types of work areas on the Team Wheel. The society's prime function was seen as certifying members, while its secondary function was seen as renewing annual memberships and ensuring that codes of conduct and standards were upheld.

Once they had paid their subscriptions, members maintained the right to use the qualifications of the society and practice their profession. They also received a monthly newsletter, a quarterly journal and an invitation to the society's annual conference.

A newly appointed director, who felt that the society needed to be more proactive, decided to establish a committee that placed more attention on Innovating and Promoting. The committee's goal was to gather ideas from members on how the society could improve its services and then set about developing the society's role accordingly.

Members responded enthusiastically, and a new series of workshops were established, not only in the technical aspects of the profession but also in the managerial ones. Other innovations taken on board included services that provided advice on issues relating to health, insurance, travel and employment. In order to ensure that these services were paid for, funds were set aside for Promoting them on a pay-as-you-use basis.

Gradually, the society began to establish a reputation for being a leader in the field, rather than just a membership organization. The original focus on Inspecting the entry to the profession was maintained, but new avenues were opened up through a major effort on Innovating and Promoting.

CASE STUDY: PRODUCING AND INNOVATING

Anyone who has worked on a car assembly line will tell you that Producing involves working to a system. There are, however, many different ways and methods of producing and delivering a service or a product.

A manufacturing engineer told me,

> You can have all the best ideas and promote the product, but if you can't produce it to the right level of quality or deliver it on time you'll go out of business.

He also noted that those involved in Producing usually want a well-structured way of doing things.

> Only when you have a well-tried system that people can use time and time again can you get your costs down and ensure a reliable output. It's my job to help establish a clear, systematic way of working, so everyone knows what they are doing on a regular basis. If we keep changing the system, we will achieve little.

Linking, Producing and Innovating

Those involved in Producing derive great satisfaction from seeing outputs and a job concluded. To them it is not a boring activity, but one in which they take great pride. The job is not complete until they can sign off and say, 'We have produced what we set out to do'.

Producing is the ability to provide what the customer wants efficiently and effectively. This is done by having systems in place to keep tasks on track, such as the ordering of materials, the sequencing of orders, and the avoidance of log-jams in the process.

Those involved in Producing often have problems with those that do not supply the materials on time or change the order halfway through the process. They also get upset with those who promote the product or who make unrealistic delivery promises that cannot be met.

Increasingly organizations are realizing the importance of improving teamwork by having those involved in the Producing area working closely with those who are mainly Innovating, to ensure closer co-operation. The Team Wheel and systems are being used in this process to help people from different functions work together effectively.

The value of opposites

I have noticed that while people want to learn more about their own work preferences, they also welcome the opportunity to learn how to work in other parts of the Team Wheel.

'I've always enjoyed the Innovating and Promoting side of the business. That's why I'm in marketing I guess,' said John Straw, a marketing manager.

> However, the Team Wheel shows me that I need to look at areas to which I previously hadn't paid much attention. The effort I have put on Maintaining and Inspecting has paid me dividends. I recognized that maintaining effective relationships with our customers is critical to success.

We need to understand the opposite of what we do at work in order to gain a complete picture. Too often, you hear people deriding the work of other's which is different to theirs. We tend to have stereotypes. This is usually an indication of poor Linking. In such situations, people have not taken the time to find out what others can contribute.

The value of analyzing opposites lies in understanding the different aspects of work, and the ways in which people can contribute. In this way the Team Wheel, as described can make a powerful impact. It explains the need for balance between the work task functions and the personal work preferences and competencies of team members.

How to assess Linking

Linking is at the heart of teamwork. It is often easy to talk about, but harder to do. However, it can be made easier if you take the time and a bit of a risk in getting everyone together, like the conductor of an orchestra who strives to have everyone understanding what each member is contributing.

EXERCISE

This is how to establish a team discussion on Linking. There are two elements:

- The first is to assess the task links between team members.
- The second is to assess the people links between team members.

Use the following chart for scoring:

	Task links	People links
Advising		
Innovating		
Promoting		
Developing		
Organizing		
Producing		
Inspecting		
Maintaining		

Circulate it to all team members. Ask them to give a score out of 10 on each item, where 0 is low and 10 is high. Then record the scores on a whiteboard.

This chart is a useful one to put up at meetings. It provides a quick checklist to assess the strong and the weak areas.

Each person in the group should indicate the facts and feelings behind their score. Once these points have been discussed, list the Linking activities that are proposed to overcome areas of weakness. In this way you can identify key areas for action. The scoring is only the basis for discussion. Focus on the issues rather than the scores. It is always valuable to get a good team discussion on important issues going, and this approach is a quick and effective means for doing so.

Summary

This chapter has looked at real case examples of how the Team Wheel can be applied, in both project management situations and in regular teams. The value of the Team Wheel is that it provides both a task view and a people view of the issues. It is no use having effective task linking, as for example in the planning, if the people side is not supporting that on a day-to-day basis. This applies, as indicated, in both internal and external Linking.

The key point is that there is no simple formula solution to Linking. It requires day-by-day attention. It is hard work to think of the cross-boundary issues, and then go out and do something about them. Proactivity at this level is an important management skill. The good news is that it deserves, and usually gains, recognition and reward.

EXERCISE

- How effective is your team in each of the key areas of the Team Wheel?
- How do you rate your personal Linking skills in relating to all the eight work function areas, and what do you need to do to improve in each area?

■ **CHAPTER THREE** ■

Advising work – how to get the relevant information

Team information skills

In this chapter, and the ones to follow, you will have the opportunity to see how the team skills and competencies apply to the eight major team work areas. Practical examples and cases illustrate the issues. You will have the chance to look at how they affect you personally, your job and your team.

Let us start with business information. Accurate, timely and relevant information is vital to any business. If important data is not available about the tasks to be performed, then decision-making will be faulty. Advising, which deals with this aspect of teamwork activity, is therefore essential to success.

All team members are involved, to varying extents, in gathering and sharing information, but some like this kind of work more than others. This means that they are likely to spend more time identifying and collecting the required information.

This contrasts with those team members who may be more impatient to get into action. They are more inclined to act on limited information as the basis for making decisions. This can still be effective, particularly if they have a lot of experience and good intuition, but equally it can be a short-cut and create problems.

A person's ability to link well with other colleagues depends on various factors, as we shall see in each of the segments of the Team Wheel. Gaining the relevant information, however, is high on the list. Your job will involve both:

■ gaining information via internal or external links
■ giving information via internal or external links.

Advising

We have asked many people what Advising means to them, and also how they use it in Linking with others. This has given us an understanding of the contribution it makes to teamwork. Here are some of the responses received. They reflect the way some people see Advising from an internal viewpoint of Linking with colleagues. Others see Advising primarily as an external action of Linking with clients:

> Every member of the team needs to be excellent on their Advising skills. I am given many opinions, but I look for the facts behind them. I therefore spend a lot of time listening to others before I get into action [project manager].

> Advising means giving our clients the best information possible in order to help them make decisions. I have to spend a considerable time internally working with colleagues before going out to meet the clients. In that sense, I am involved in both internal and external Linking [financial advisor].

> I try to find out what the patient regards as the main symptoms, and then conduct an assessment, so that I can provide the best prescription to treat the problem. From time to time, if it is a complex problem, I will consult with other colleagues for their opinion [my doctor].

These are examples from different industries and work areas. In each, the importance of Advising is recognized. This is increasingly so in the modern world, where it is rare for one person to have all the data required to resolve an issue. Those who provide the best advice invariably have the best network, and are often the most effective at Linking.

Increasingly, much of that information comes from Linking with people whom you may never meet. For example, the world of the Web enables you to contact people all over the world, to exchange ideas and information, and specialized networks are part of professional Linking.

Everyone is involved in Advising, but two professions in particular make their living primarily in that way – lawyers and accountants. I discussed this with my own lawyer and accountant. Their views are interesting:

Lawyer

> As a lawyer, the central aspect of my work is giving my clients advice based on what the law says in relation to the particular issues. In many cases this is very difficult, as it is a matter of interpretation, and the client may not always appreciate that by being cautious I am acting in their best interest. At the end of the day, the value of my contribution is in the quality of the advice I give to my client. In that sense, I am often involved as a third party, and therefore a link, between people in conflict as well as having links to other colleagues in the profession.

Accountant

> My job is to gather and sift through both the hard financial data, and also business information related to how things are produced and sold. It involves a close contact with various colleagues in other parts of the business. I had not previously seen this as an important Linking function, but that is what I spend a lot of time doing. Based on this information, I then have to provide reports and give advice on how best to make decisions about the business.

Each of these examples reflects different aspects of giving advice, and the associated Linking activities involved. In short, there are two key aspects to any job:

- The technical aspects, which is what people normally think of when they get professional advice.
- The process and interpersonal aspects, which are essential in order to gain the data and form a view, and respond in an appropriate way.

The first is the Advising function, and the second is the Linking activity. Therefore, the Advising function covers a range of team task activities both internally and externally. A team cannot make the right decisions without good Advising skills, and it is vital that each member of the team takes this work function seriously, but equally focusses on their links, which will determine to a large extent how well their advice is accepted. It is the leader's job to show an example in these areas.

Advising on projects

A considerable amount of teamwork these days involves projects. The first stage of any project is to get a comprehensive brief on the current situation and objectives. This is where Advising starts, and your success will depend on the questions you pose, and the answers you gain during the brief.

Some of the advice you need may be general strategic information, such as:

- What are the goals?
- Who are the stakeholders?
- What are the boundaries?

Other aspects will be more specific, such as:

- What are the critical deadline times?
- What are the investment limits and cost budgets?
- What outputs are required?

It is often tempting to move into action before understanding the problems and processes. A key aspect of leadership is to ensure that first things come first. It is here that the skills of gaining the appropriate advice is required – both in terms of asking the right questions and knowing who should provide the answers. Let us look at some aspects of Advising, and the Linking skills implications.

The changing focus

Information technology

Traditionally those involved in Advising were usually seen as information support players, the 'backroom' people. The production, sales and marketing departments were seen as the places of action. Today, those ideas are changing. The Advising role in teams is becoming increasingly important as the basis of future success. Research is now a strategic competitive weapon, and IT is leading the revolution.

The advent of the computer, fax, and now the electronic transmission of information via the Internet, is taking the information and Advising function to the leading edge. It is crucial to decision-making.

The value of the information lies in its application. It is here that Linking skills are important, particularly amongst information technologists, some of whom have been criticized for not communicating well with colleagues and clients.

Real-time Advising

The introduction of network arrangements between people who need to share information has speeded up communications. People working together in teams and on projects no longer need to be in the same room, building or city.

The nature of the network system enables people to communicate in an introverted way with people who are separated by many thousands of miles. There are teams, like our own TMS organization, which have members in Australia, Europe and America. Their main communication is conducted daily through the satellite networks, and they only meet occasionally.

There are dangers in this because the personal links can break down. The advent of the computer camera and instant face-to-face electronic chat is one way in which interpersonal Linking is being strengthened in the cyber age.

CASE STUDIES

I asked many people about their Advising role, and it is interesting to see how modern technology is influencing their work.

Librarian Ros Fernandez works in a major library. She said,

> As a librarian, I've seen major changes in the way in which we relate to our clients. Yes, our key role is Advising, but we are becoming the guides to the technology of communication, rather than giving the advice personally.
>
> Our work is mainly showing our clients how to gain access to the electronic information systems. Increasingly it has become a do-it-yourself system instead of asking the librarian to look up the information. Our own teamwork and training is changing from information management and transmission to information education and facilitation. This puts more emphasis on the personal communication and delegation aspects, where Linking is important.

It is interesting to see how the work of the medical profession is also beginning to change. Increasingly most doctors have patient information on their computer. Also on their computers they have additional information about symptoms and diagnoses and the latest research on certain diseases. They can also access lists of specialists for easy referrals. This all helps the advice they provide and the speed at which they can do it.

My own doctor now regularly refers to his computer in the process of his analysis of symptoms. After being in hospital, I visited him and mentioned the drug they gave me for a kidney infection. He said it was new to him, but immediately identified it on his computer and discussed the side-effects it could have. This kind of instant advice based on technology is increasingly part of what is expected in all teams and projects.

'View-and-do' meetings

I have encouraged my consulting clients to improve their performance by having sessions in which they concentrate on giving and receiving advice to and from each other. I call these 'view-and-do' meetings. This can be done by having a bulletin board on which people can post information or questions or issues. Then a time is set to discuss the points and resolve the issues. It raises the energy level and leads to quick improvements.

Some project teams that are all on the same site have a system in which the team can meet for 10 or 15 minutes each morning and evening to share and compare their views about the operations. This is increasingly the system used by various manufacturing organizations in factories.

In these meetings they quickly indicate problems and opportunities, which can then be followed up by those concerned. It is this kind of quick Linking process that has led to improved performance through good information, good sharing and good advice.

A variant on this, for project teams all on one site, is the 10–15-minute 'stand up' meeting, where project team leaders meet to share their thoughts for the day. When they go back as Linkers to their own teams, they run their own 'stand up' meeting in which the information is shared with their team members. In this way, information can pass up and down the organization quickly.

These are clear examples of team leaders acting as interface Linking representatives of their team by external Linking, where they actively listen, communicate and problem-solve on the issues.

Advising processes

The Advising process covers two main areas: gathering information and giving information. It is what we call 'green' work because it fits in the green section of the Team Wheel and because green is the colour of quiet reflection.

To do its job effectively, a team needs to gather all the relevant information associated with the work of the team. This means:

- reading reports, books, journals and newspapers
- understanding industry trends and statistics
- keeping up with legislation
- keeping a record of the financial situation
- attending conferences and seminars to keep up to date.

Someone should have the responsibility for being the 'linker of key information', ensuring that accurate, relevant information is always available to the team. This will involve people posting their latest news on the intranet, or organizing meetings, so that people can understand and contribute to developments.

How well does your team do on these Advising functions?

Networks

It is increasingly important to have extensive external personal networks to gain good advice, ones in which you can regularly meet with people from other organizations to learn what is happening elsewhere. A good way to extend your external Linking is by becoming a member of other business-related organizations, such as clubs and professional societies.

Some teams like to 'trade' information with other teams. Sharing team information with other people and key stakeholders opens the doors for return information. In other words, 'the more you give, the more you get'. Therefore making presentations at conferences can enhance both the standing of your organization and that of your own role and career.

These are all ways in which your external Linking can lead to useful connections that would not otherwise occur.

Linking information flows in teams

The Advising process in teams needs to be two-way, with information about organizational goals and priorities readily provided to the team. Team members need to know that their ideas are heard. The process therefore must ensure that there is a mechanism for ideas to be passed on to senior management.

Often the people who know most about current problems are those working at the 'coalface'. A good Advising function will establish a mechanism for team members to comment upon existing problems and opportunities. However, too often that is missing, and the lessons of experience are ignored and turn to criticism through neglect.

The Team Wheel provides a ready-made checklist to aid discussions. On many occasions we have had project meetings where the Team Wheel has been the framework for discussion. It is amazing how quickly people get to the point after focussing on an area of the Wheel. Here are some examples from consulting cases of how the Types of Work model has been used. It helps people focus their energies on issues, and provides a common language for problem-solving:

The new product team

> We have done a good job on the Organizing and Producing sides, but we need to improve on the Inspecting aspects.

The person making this comment was invited to give examples and to suggest ways of tackling the problem. He did so. He used the terms of the Team Wheel to review the situation, and that showed the value of having a common language for discussing the issues.

> We are rushing into Organizing and Producing before we have spent sufficient time in the Advising and Developing phases.

This criticism, supported by others, was the basis of concern expressed by a team member. The result was a review of operations.

Another member said,

> I am concerned with the way we are Producing and Maintaining our products, as I can see we are taking too many short-cuts.

This comment led to an action research study of the procedures and processes, and the improvement of operating systems. In this the major activity was bringing people together to discuss the issues and develop better ways of doing things. They were the same people, but the difference was the process of Linking to enable them to advise each other in a positive spirit.

CASE STUDY: PURCHASING

One of the most interesting examples of teamwork is a team involved in the Advising phase of materials purchasing for a large petrochemical plant.

Previously, the materials orders were planned and agreed upon with the purchasing manager at regular meetings. These meetings were often lengthy, as a great deal of information was discussed regarding market trends and current availability. Once the materials orders were filled, the stock-control manager would contact each department by phone, arrange meetings and ensure that the various orders were properly distributed. This system took time, and communication problems often occurred.

The organization introduced a new purchasing system in which the pricing and delivery of all materials was available on networked computers in each department. The purchasing department was responsible for updating this information, and also adding new listings of products from new suppliers.

At the meetings, everyone indicated what they wanted and when. As a result, the meeting time was halved and the numbers of disagreements were markedly reduced. In addition to streamlining the purchasing process, an arrangement was also made with many of the suppliers to store the ordered materials until required, on the basis of a 24-hour notice of delivery. This concept was very successful, and warehousing facilities and costs were substantially reduced.

The purchasing managers developed this process. By analyzing the information that they needed, and finding a fast efficient means of receiving it, they discovered they could improve their efficiency in buying and distributing resources. This resulted in considerable time and cost savings. Again, it was not just the Advising that led to improvements, but the process of Linking between the various people.

CASE STUDY: THE LEGAL TEAM

A small legal team of three lawyers and two support staff carried out a process analysis on the Advising processes in their team. A process flow diagram, drawn up for one particular project, showed that there was considerable inefficiency in how information was gathered and distributed.

One lawyer worked on part of the project, requesting the support staff to gather information from libraries and other parts of the law firm. The job would then be passed onto another lawyer in the team for her specialized input. She would request further information from the same support staff, who then had to revisit the library. The support staff spent much of their time doing this when one visit would have sufficed, had an information flow diagram been drawn up.

As a result of this analysis the team was able to become more efficient in its advisory work. In this case, co-ordination was improved by focussing on task Linking issues such as objective-setting, work allocation and delegation issues.

Working with independent consulting advisers

Advisers come in all shapes and sizes, from finance consultants to medical doctors and all sorts of other professions. As a team leader, what can be done to make sure the relationships work? The important thing in working with them effectively is to give them a good brief. That means that before you start to talk to them you need to think through what you want them to do. Providing a written statement of objectives is a good starting-point.

Many people who prefer the advisory role find it hard to work to a strict timetable and system. Also, many Advisers who are independent base their work around their personal lifestyle, and that does not always fit well with traditional organizational life.

To ensure that you get a good working relationship, let them know not only what you do, but why, and what assistance you are likely to want from them. In particular, indicate:

- the outputs
- the timetable
- a budget.

Advisers are often caring people, but make sure that they do not spend too much time researching and not enough on delivery.

Advising skills

The Advising function is important in business, as 'action' is only a follow-up to information that has been well gathered, shared, thought through and discussed. Those professionals who have spent many years giving advice, such as lawyers, accountants and librarians, have a lot to offer other professions who are now taking this area of teamwork more seriously. As a team leader, you can learn a lot from them.

Professionals who spend a lot of time advising have told us that they see 'asking the right questions' as the main factor contributing to their success. While 'asking the right questions' requires experience, it is nevertheless a skill that people can develop.

This skill involves analyzing the information processes by using the '5-W' technique. For example:

- WHAT information do we need?
- WHY do we need it?
- WHERE do we get it?
- WHO will get it?
- WHEN do we need it?

Applications

Try these steps for improving the Advising function in your teamwork.

- Ask each team member to list the areas on the Team Wheel that they feel need attention.
- Ask for examples and evidence.
- Discover whether there are gaps in the information and where they are.
- Ask who will take responsibility for discovering what is required.
- Follow up, at an agreed date, with a meeting in which the issues are discussed.

In addition, look at what information the team passes on to others. Who else in the organization might benefit from the information the team has? Can a bilateral information exchange agreement be established with sources external to the team?

On the external side, review which societies and professional groups your team members belong to. Encourage sharing, so that those team members can bring back information from different sources. Most importantly, make sure that there is a process for disseminating all this information.

In so doing, you will find the quality of decisions improving and the spirit and energy of those involved rising, as members begin to recognize that they are part of a truly professional project team.

Summary

This chapter has outlined the importance of the Advising work function in any team. Information is increasingly a key asset of any team and organization. Modern technology allows the capture and manipulation of that information, but it requires a high level of professionalism to identify the data required in the first place.

This is where team members involved in this part of the work need to focus on Linking with those who have access to the data and those who know how it should be used.

As with all aspects of the Team Wheel, each person needs to understand their role in each work function. This means a work situation in which people can contribute their knowledge proactively, rather than waiting to be asked. Successful team leaders create an environment in which this positive criticism is encouraged.

> **EXERCISE**
>
> - In your current work, to what extent do you rate the extent to which you, as the team leader, are effective in the Advising area?
> - How effective is your team in its Advising work, and what specific links need establishing to improve things?

■ **CHAPTER FOUR** ■

Innovating work – creating ideas and experimenting

Keys to creative teamwork

It was originally suggested that the computer would make life easier. In many respects it has. It has also speeded up the pace of change, and the pace of work.

No organization is now safe unless it continually innovates. Microsoft Corporation, which has led many changes in the last decade, acknowledges that most of its products will be obsolete within three years, unless it continually updates. Therefore, the Innovating function of the Team Wheel is vital in every organization.

In times past, when things moved more slowly, everyone had more time to ensure that all the parts and activities fitted together. Today, top-class Linking is essential to keep innovation on track.

The work function of Innovating has become a key word in organizations. It is not just the grand R&D innovation on new products. It is innovating at all levels, including each and every job. The reason that project management has taken off with such force is that it is the only way to involve people with the skills and knowledge in a participative process of rapid change.

This chapter provides ways and means of improving the Innovating process in conjunction with Linking skills and competencies. This is essential if innovations are to succeed. Too often in the past innovation has failed because those involved did not put sufficient effort into Linking. They assumed that the ideas and innovations would speak for themselves.

How to start Innovating

Let us start by reviewing some practical examples and the learning points arising. The most important thing is that everyone needs to know what they are expected to contribute to the Innovating process. That is different from everyone doing their own thing. There needs to be an approach that people understand.

At Toyota, the starting-point is the suggestion-box system. All employees are invited to put forward suggestions for improvements. People are rewarded if their suggestions are adopted. This is a simple but effective way of letting everyone know that their ideas are welcome and providing a way in which they can contribute.

3M, in the US, is renowned for its focus on innovation. Again, each staff member is encouraged to allocate time to thinking and contributing new ideas.

The important thing about innovation is that it invariably has a systems knock-on effect. If you change something in one job, or one task, or one area then it will have an impact on other jobs, tasks and areas. That is why teamwork, and a language for the sharing of team innovations, is crucial.

In order to improve a team's efforts, it is important to come up with new ideas and develop them into action. Some managers do this naturally, by setting aside time for people to criticize in a positive way how things are being done.

CASE STUDY

The approach of Wayne Bennet, the manager of a factory that makes cardboard boxes, is a good example. He asked me to consult with his organization because he said, 'We need some new ideas and innovation to improve performance'.

Wayne's team was extremely practical, concentrating mainly on the Organizing and Producing functions of the Team Wheel. At our first meeting, Wayne said,

> We never seem to come up with new ways of doing things. Some of our procedures have been in place for 10 years, and we have been very slow to computerize traditional ways of doing administrative work.

I suggested running a workshop with the focus on 'new ways of running the factory'. He arranged for his supervisors and administrative staff to meet for two hours after the shiftwork for the day had finished. I asked them what they felt were the main issues to consider if they were going to reduce costs and improve productivity. They soon had a list on the board, although some of the items were surprising.

I then introduced the Team Wheel. I explained how the eight key work functions could make the difference between a high-performing team and a low-performing one. In the discussion on strengths and weaknesses, the team agreed that it executed the Organizing, Producing and Inspecting functions very well but they definitely scored low on Innovating.

They felt that this was a team problem, not a lack of individual ideas. Therefore, at the meeting each member of the team was asked to put forward one idea of how the factory operations could be improved on the issues listed. They quickly came up with 15 ideas. Each one of them was discussed by the team.

The process used was straightforward. Each person who put an idea forward had to indicate why it was important, and what benefits could be gained by tackling it. Wherever they gained support, a project team was formed on a volunteer basis to investigate the idea.

Amazing results occurred. Within three months, over $250,000 had been saved! The team began to make real improvements, not only on the financial side, but also in the way they worked together.

The people were the same as before. They were doing the same jobs as before. But suddenly they were generating ideas and putting them into action. They were not only Innovating, but applying their innovations in a way that they had not done before. Why?

Firstly they were given permission to share and compare ideas in a team meeting. Secondly they started discussing ways and means of Innovating and how to make it work. Thirdly they started Linking in new ways. They linked in small trio teams to research the ideas. They Linked by going out to clients and suppliers. For example, one team compared the terms of different suppliers in order to negotiate better purchasing terms. They Linked by going to their own staff and getting them involved and excited. They Linked by finding information. They Linked more closely with their manager to get action.

In short, they understood the power of Innovating and Linking working hand-in-hand. The original innovation ideas were mainly technical and task-orientated suggestions. The process for assessing and implementing them was based on interpersonal Linking.

The result was that after the sixth monthly meeting Wayne rang me and asked, 'Would it be all right if you don't come to the next meeting?'

'Sure,' I said. 'Why is that?'

Wayne replied, 'I think I now have the idea of what we should be doing'.

He became the chief Linker in the team.

Learning points and guidelines

The success of this team indicates the importance of having planned and held regular Innovating sessions. Wayne had not been arranging such meetings. After watching me do it as a consultant, and using the Team Wheel as the key tool to help the team understand what to do, he took on the role himself.

These meetings are information exchanges, and should be set up so that team members can work in an uninterrupted way. There are several points to consider when arranging such sessions:

- Involve people in discussing how and when the session will take place, rather than just instructing them to turn up.
- Establish a set of guidelines, so that ideas can be freely put forward and not immediately 'shot down' by people who oppose them.
- Assist people in understanding the Team Wheel.
- Give each person a personal Team Management Profile, which is the feedback on their own team work preferences (see appendix).
- Discuss the team model with everyone, as it helps structure and guide the discussion.
- Write up and record all ideas, regardless of how 'way out' they may seem.
- Seek the facts to support an idea whenever it is put forward, rather than knock it down simply on the basis of opinion. This usually means an off-site meeting for at least a day, or often longer.
- Nurture a creative atmosphere. It is in this kind of supportive environment that people are able to put forward good ideas, as well as ones they are not sure about.

The Innovating process

A supportive atmosphere encourages ideas that can be built on, and these in turn can lead to truly novel approaches. However, Innovating is quite often a difficult process for some team members. It is not simply a matter of saying, 'Tomorrow morning I'll spend some time Innovating'. It is more of a process, and needs to be built into the very fabric of the team.

The team leader of a well-known design group in Europe said, 'In our team we encourage people to ask, "Why are we doing things this way?" Our innovations have come about by people analyzing how tasks are carried out in the home and then asking why we cannot make something to assist.'

Usually innovation doesn't just happen – it is the result of many hours of thinking, reading and sharing ideas with others. In other words it is hard work. Nevertheless, Innovating is a skill that can be developed by everyone.

Innovation requires:

■ an open mind
■ an orientation to the future
■ an ability to gather information
■ a willingness to listen to and consult with others
■ a determination to keep up with state-of-the-art technology in the key technical areas of the job.
■ a recognition that Linking with others is crucial to success.

Often individuals in teams are resistant to change. 'We've always done it this way' is a common response we receive. However, technology is moving at such a fast rate that new processes are often superseded as they are installed. People who get locked into the past will pay the penalty of not being competitive in the future.

Imagination

Our research has shown that people who find it easy to 'imagine' generate ideas more readily. This means that they have the ability to think in pictures or to fantasize. These visual processes can be stimulated and developed within a team in order to get the best Innovating result.

This is done by skilled Linking to bring people together and facilitate positive discussion. This stimulation of the creative senses can be done by exercises such as:

- What does the future market for our product look like?
- Draw a picture of how you see things changing.
- What does the product of tomorrow have to feel like?

The Innovating process combines the power of people thinking ideas through on their own with the energy, enthusiasm and stimulation that comes from a brain-storming session with their fellow team members. The Linking that takes place in such meetings is often taken for granted. When a team is performing poorly in the Innovating area it is invariably the case that the Linking is absent. In short, no-one calls people together for that purpose. If people do come together, there is no-one facilitating via active listening and focussing on communications. Linking can make the difference between high innovation and low innovation levels.

CASE STUDY

In my research on innovation I interviewed John Nicholas, an operations manager in the manufacturing plant described in the earlier case. He said,

> We were so busy keeping the operations line going to meet our targets, we never took time to look at how we innovated. If we had kept going in that direction, we would have missed new opportunities for our business.
>
> As a result of the Innovating meetings at all levels, we now concentrate on ideas for improvement. We concentrate on reviewing the best ideas. We have gained from applying some good ones, particularly in the area of just-in-time management of our raw materials.

Success requires this positive approach to innovation. It has to be on the agenda. It has to be allocated time and money. It has to be taken seriously by the team leader. If these things are in place, the team members will take innovation seriously.

Innovative people

People who are skilled in Innovating work have a number of important characteristics, including the ability to focus on 'what could be', rather than 'what is'. They also:

- challenge conventional ways of doing things
- bring a high level of curiosity and questioning to the job
- enjoy testing ideas
- are future orientated
- prefer to look beyond traditional frames of reference
- bring new insights to ways of tackling problems and opportunities.

Therefore, if you have people like that in your team, think twice before you reject what they say. They may be pointing the way to the future but have little evidence to show. That is the reason for appointing a project group to assess the ideas.

Many people who are strong on Innovating describe themselves as being:

- ideas people
- flexible and willing to change if a better idea comes up rather than working to a formula
- sometimes not well organized, liking to keep many things within easy reach
- experimenters
- often absorbed in their work, perhaps to the exclusion of other things
- able to work best when they have what they think is a great idea
- perhaps forgetful on certain practical issues because they focus on their ideas
- sometimes sceptical
- often misunderstood because of their unconventional ways.

They enjoy spending time developing theories or models, and researching issues in depth before moving into action. They rely heavily on their intuition and ability to think beyond what exists to 'what might be'.

While some people are naturally innovative, others can learn the skills. Creative thinking courses or workshops can help you develop these skills. There are books on lateral thinking and imagineering. However, the one thing that is essential, and not usually covered in the books and courses, are the skills of Linking.

Innovating without Linking rarely succeeds. Innovative thinking flourishes where it is encouraged.

Everyone can come up with innovative ideas if they have experience of the subject under discussion. Some people may have more of a preference for this kind of work, but in a project group invite everyone to contribute to the process of Innovating.

A model of Innovation

The Wallas paradigm (Wallas, 1926), was introduced to me by my colleague Dick McCann, who provided the following notes. Wallas proposed that the creative process consists of four components, and helps us understand the nature of innovative thinking:

- preparation
- incubation
- illumination
- verification.

Preparation

This phase requires the gathering of all possible information concerning a problem. It can be obtained through reading, attending conferences and consulting with others so as to gather as much data as possible. In addition, it is important to have the intent and resolve to come up with a truly innovative approach. This requires the constant examining of a problem, visualizing scenarios of possible solutions, and gathering even the most tangential of facts that might be relevant to the problem.

The composer Strauss once said, 'I can tell you from my own experience that an ardent desire and a fixed purpose, combined with an intense inner resolve brings results. Determined concentrated thought is a tremendous force…I am convinced that this is a law, and it holds good in any line of endeavour.'

Incubation

The incubation mode is the period in which the mind 'ticks over', trying to piece together the various bits of information. It may involve forgetting the problem for a while, or passing it over to the unconscious while the conscious mind goes off-line into relaxation, daydreaming, a meditative state, or even sleep.

The 1936 Nobel Prize winner Otto Loewi reported:

The night before Easter Sunday of that year (1920) I awoke, turned on the light and jotted down a few notes on a tiny slip of thin paper. Then I fell asleep again. It occurred to me at six o'clock in the morning that during the night I had written down something important, but I was unable to decipher the scrawl. The next night, at three o'clock, the idea returned. It was the design of an experiment to determine whether or not the hypothesis of chemical transmission that I had uttered 17 years ago was correct. I got up immediately, went to the laboratory, and performed a simple experiment on a frog's heart according to the nocturnal design. Its results became the foundation of the theory of chemical transmission of the nervous impulse.

Illumination

The illumination stage is the 'output' of the innovation, and will often occur as a flash of inspiration, seemingly coming from nowhere, but actually the result of many hours of unconscious incubation.

The famous scientist Kekule, who discovered the benzene ring in chemistry, said in his famous lecture towards the end of his career:

> I turned my chair to the fire and dozed. Again the atoms were gambolling before my eyes. This time the smaller groups kept modestly in the background. My mental eye, rendered more acute by repeated visions of this kind, could now distinguish larger structures of manifold conformation: long rows, sometimes more closely fitted together; all twining and twisting in snakelike motion. But look! What was that? One of the snakes had seized hold of its own tail, and the form whirled mockingly before my eyes. As if by the flash of lightning I awoke. Let us learn to dream, gentlemen.

Verification

The verification phase is the reality check to make sure that the innovation is workable and practical. As Mendeleev, who devised the periodic table in chemistry, reported in 1869:

> I went to bed exhausted after struggling to conceptualize a way to categorize the elements based upon their atomic weights. I saw in a dream a table where all the elements fell into place as required. Awakening, I immediately wrote it down on a piece of paper. Only in one place did a correction later seem necessary.

Working with Innovators

It can at times be difficult to work with Innovators. They often 'march to the beat of their own drum'. The key factor in their lives is their ideas. They pursue these relentlessly, but not always in an organized way. They dislike too many systems and constraints. Yet in order to move innovations forward, they need some form of system and organization.

There are extroverted and introverted Innovators. The former often think out loud, and enjoy informal meetings to share and compare ideas. The introverted Innovators prefer to work more by themselves. They may be reluctant to share ideas until they have worked upon them, and shown that they have some substance.

Working with Innovators requires patience, because they like a flexible approach. They dislike being tied strictly to time or budgetary constraints. So, depending on your preference, work out how best to link with Innovators. A first step is to ask them how they prefer to work, and tell them how you operate. Then, establish some mutual guidelines. It sounds straightforward. Though more difficult in practice, it can prevent major communication problems later on.

Innovating within teams

I have always found that the Innovating process with a team is enhanced by the use of a whiteboard. Team members should be encouraged to record their ideas in visual format so that everyone can see what they are thinking. Visual data will trigger the internal visual channel in each person, and enhance their own creativity.

Ideas should first be listed without comment, and then grouped together. Only after all ideas are on the board should an analysis be carried out to prioritize the data. This stops ideas being knocked down before they have been considered. It also ensures all ideas are circulated, rather than having some members feeling that their contribution has not been heard, and therefore switching off by not listening to other contributions.

Project groups can then be assigned to the important ideas, as the above examples show. The whole process of individual thinking, combined with group effort, can lead to major results over a period of time.

The four stages of preparation, incubation, illumination and verification are easily taught, and can be a great aid to innovation. Individual creativity can in this way be synthesized with the power of group processes to make the team truly effective.

How to innovate on projects

Here are some ideas to enable you and your team to concentrate on Innovating:

- Look at existing ways of doing things, and involve others, to consider what improvements could be made.
- Question assumptions and opinions, in a positive way, by looking for ways of testing them.
- Look for connections between ideas, and see how they can work together.
- To make sure ideas are not forgotten, write them down.
- Ensure all key words and phrases are written on a whiteboard, so that everyone can see and hear what is happening.
- Call Innovating meetings when you have a major problem, and involve those who have a contribution, whatever their level in the organization.
- Make sure you follow through on the innovative ideas in your Linking role to gain action in other areas of the Team Wheel.

EXERCISE

- How do you get your best ideas? Is it by practical involvement in a task, by reading, by watching, by listening, by spending time alone?
- How can you improve the innovation of your team?

CHAPTER FIVE

Promoting work – selling the message

Communicating with the stakeholders

How well does your organization promote its products and services? Is it done well or poorly? I have discussed this with many people in organizations, and am usually surprised by the results.

Promoting is not one activity but many. It involves:

- establishing the right image
- the merchandising and presentation of the products and services
- the demonstration of the products and services
- communicating the features and benefits at all levels
- making the personal contacts and representations
- networking and exploring new opportunities for sales.

Some people see promotions just as sales. That is not so. Sales should be the result of effective Promoting. Selling is vital to any business, as indeed is the marketing that goes behind it. Promoting combines both.

Promoting is done by everyone, albeit some people do not like to see themselves in that light. We all have to promote ourselves to get a job. We should be interested in promoting our careers. If we are in a leadership position, we will promote certain people to positions ahead of others. In short, Promoting means pushing things forward by presenting them in a way that is acceptable.

All team members that I interviewed recognized the importance of getting their message across to clients and key stakeholders, both internally and externally. However, many found promoting their service or product a difficult thing to do.

Linking and Promoting

Anyone involved in Promoting needs also to spend time Linking. This involves bringing various people and activities together, for example talking with clients or customers. It may be Linking with an advertising agency to discuss a campaign. It may be discussing sponsorship. It can equally mean presenting at a conference. These are external Promoting links.

However, internal Linking is equally important to the promotion of the work that you and your team do. Many individuals and teams do good work, but do not receive the recognition they deserve because they do not promote their work well. This can reflect itself, at the personal level, in low recognition and slow advancement. At the team level, it can result in a reduced budget and reduction in staff.

In this chapter we will, therefore, look at examples of Promoting, and show how it can work more effectively with effective links.

Images and action

In a consulting project, I was involved in an image study of a postal service. The Chief Executive had the view that although the postal service was doing a good job it was also vital to communicate this to the general public. He set up a special project task force to discover the public's view of the organization, and how it compared internationally with other postal services. This manager put a high premium on Linking with his customers, and using the Promoting area to enhance it.

Once the results were collated, they initiated a major new campaign to communicate the work of the organization, under the banner 'We deliver'. This involved a major promotion to customers on the wider role of the postal service. Subsequent customer surveys showed an increased satisfaction rating. There was also a marked increase in the sales figures. This success was a direct result of the organization promoting its services more effectively.

Promoting is the total process by which all members of an organization communicate on a regular basis their work and service. In this case, members of the postal service gained higher self-esteem and a feeling that they were more appreciated by their customers as a result of the new image and messages.

Promoting priorities

The great value of the Team Wheel is that it provides an easy-to-use vehicle to assess priorities. By giving each of the eight areas a score out of ten, for the effort put into each segment, you can quickly get a feel for the importance attached to it.

Often the weight of effort goes into the problems, not the opportunities. For example, when something is going well it may be relatively ignored, and the attention goes elsewhere. This is dangerous, particularly if it relates to Promoting.

Some products and services may sell themselves, but they are very few and far between. It has always been interesting to ask people how they regard Promoting, and what priority they place on it in their business. Here are some responses.

CASE STUDIES

John Blake, an accountant in a medium-sized practice involved with one of our companies, said,

> Most of my work involves analyzing the facts and figures associated with a client's account. I find it difficult to put aside specific time for promoting my services, as it is not part of the tradition of this profession.
>
> We have always attracted most of our clients through referrals, but today it is competitive, and we have to promote the services we offer in different ways. I am now attending a workshop on how to develop our business, and I will have to allocate more time to this aspect of our work on a day-to-day basis.

While working with a manufacturing team, I discussed how well they promoted what they did. The manager said,

> We leave it to our marketing department to promote the product. Our job is to produce it. However, we do have some internal problems, as many people in the organization do not fully realize what we do. I guess it's our fault because we don't promote ourselves well internally.

Both of these instances illustrate the fact that Promoting had a low priority. It also reflects that the both leaders were not putting effort in their Linking effort in the right places. Yet, both of them recognized it as a weakness. Once it is recognized that there is a gap, it is vital that all team members put time into Promoting to effect improvements.

Representation as external Linking

Each member of a team is a representative who can communicate the work of the team clearly to others. They can do this both formally and informally. In so doing, they are acting as external Linkers.

Team members can either sit on committees or belong to task forces or project groups at some time during the course of the year. These activities provide an ideal opportunity for them to represent and promote, not only their own work but their team's as well.

By their very presence, they are acting as a representative. Whether they deliberately go out to promote their work or not, people will create an image about what they are doing. If you act as a representative of a team, it is vital that you are well prepared with information about your team's activities. It is equally important that, when asked to comment, you articulate clearly what your team is doing, and how it relates to other aspects of the organization's work. After all, an incomplete report that is poorly argued, or lacking in basic thought, sends out a poor impression to others.

CASE STUDY

Here is an example of a success story. A computer support team in a major telecommunications organization was in danger of having its budget cut by 30 per cent in the next round of departmental allocations. When it carried out a process analysis, using the Team Wheel, it discovered the reason for the proposed cut. Team members realized they were not Promoting what they were doing. They had assumed that if they did a good job they would be recognized. In reality, however, nobody in senior management really knew what this particular team did.

None of the team members considered the Promoting process a priority either, so consequently each one missed out on many opportunities to act as a positive representative of the team. The results of the analysis, however, propelled them into reviewing the situation. The team as a whole put more effort into its Promoting activities. Dramatic improvements followed. Members conducted a series of weekly 'Discovery' seminars, which explained their support services. They published a colourful monthly news bulletin, using their existing computers, which promoted their work within the organization.

Three months later the proposed 30 per cent reduced allocation was reversed – to a 5 per cent increase.

Informal promotion

When a member of the team talks informally to colleagues, perhaps at a lunch or social function, others pick up cues, clues and messages about the team and its projects. What they say gives the perception and image of how things are going.

By indicating particular successes, achievements or failures, they create impressions for others. These perceptions affect the way in which other people in the organization will regard that individual and their team. These perceptions can also influence the way in which they will relate to them in the future.

Promoting can be either negative or positive. What impact would the following comments have? Here are some short excerpts from conversations.

CASE STUDIES

1 – A project team member to a colleague, who is not on the project, but who is influential in the provision of funds to the project: 'We seem to be wasting a lot of time on the unimportant parts. Everyone is talking and no-one seems to listen. I think the project will not deliver on time.'

2 – A manager at a conference talking to a person from a client organization: 'Our organization is having a lot of computer problems at the moment. We are trying to get everyone onto the same system. It is causing lots of delays. I think the guy in charge is not up to the job.'

Such statements do not in themselves say a lot, but they do start to put doubt in people's minds. They do convey a negative image. If the listeners have power in their organization, such comments can lead to the loss of business.

Negative promotion

The following incident occurred in a takeover deal. I was personally involved as a director of the company in receipt of a good offer for its shares. It may seem bizarre, but this is what happened. The directors of both companies met and agreed the terms. Everyone signed the legal document for the sale of the company, except the Chairman. He said he would sign after he had taken the proposed new owners out to dinner. Over a good meal, where the wine flowed to celebrate the occasion, the buyers began to talk about what they would do with the company. They mentioned reducing costs and making major changes, and there was talk of staff cuts.

This diverged from the Chairman's assumptions of what would happen, and he thought it contrary to the interests of the staff, many of whom were his friends. He changed his mind. The deal required a unanimous vote of the board. By refusing to sign, the Chairman exercised his veto. Next day, he informed the buyers, to their amazement, that the deal was off. Their conversation at the dinner was negative promotion, and it killed the deal.

This proves once again that a deal is never done until it is done, and the impact of loose talk can undo months of promotion and negotiation.

Informal comments can be just as vital in Promoting as formal representations. They all create images, sometimes negative ones, as in the cases above. It is important that team members are aware of that when talking to others. Each member wields considerable influence over the way in which their team is viewed. This can have a big impact when, for example, it comes to the annual allocation of budgets and overall performance assessments.

Promoting preferences and practices

While everyone needs to understand how to promote, not everyone enjoys the up-front Promoting kind of work. However, we have found from our research that those who welcome this kind of challenge are likely to:

- be more extroverted and willing to meet new people
- enjoy putting forward their views, and be able to find out what others are interested in
- be often strong on ideas, and able to get others enthusiastic about them
- have strong views and convictions, which guide what they say and do
- have beliefs and principles that underline their confidence

- be willing to take a risk on the possibility of rejection in Promoting their ideas.

These people look for Promoting kind of jobs. Others who are quieter, less willing to speak out, and may be more concerned about rejection can nevertheless work as Promoters. But they will need to put in more effort to do so, as it is not their natural inclination.

Promoting involves many things:

- knowledge of the products and services
- skills in presenting to others ideas and services
- a positive attitude
- ability to tolerate rejection and ambiguity
- willingness to explore new territories and opportunities.

However, everyone can learn the basic principles of Promoting, which involves everything from exploring for opportunities to creating the appropriate image and persuasion. Your customers and clients look to those kind of things. So, while work preferences can and do play a big part, it is your day-to-day behaviour that makes the difference.

Stakeholders

Some people do not recognize, or value, the extent to which promotions, if done well, can impact on an organization's internal relationships. In one of the organizations mentioned, I spent time identifying key stakeholders. The team identified 16 stakeholders. They then audited how they promoted to each of them. After looking at the details, and discovering various problems, they decided to establish a promotion plan and allocate time to getting their message across to the right people. The results showed improved relationships and business.

In contrast, I have also worked with teams that felt that they were doing an excellent Promoting job. Team members told me great stories of how they influenced clients and customers. They showed me the classy advertising materials they used. However, I found out from the clients that the glossy brochures and fine words did not meet their needs. Most of the expensive material was put in the waste bin. I therefore encouraged the team members to meet regularly with their customers to gain feedback on how their 'promotions' were received, and act on the messages received.

CASE STUDIES: CUSTOMER VISITS AND SALES VISITS

One practical project involved senior managers going out to see major customers for the first time.

The customers' perceptions, and the issues they wanted to raise, surprised the managers. As a result, they were able to give their teams clearer guidance on what had to be done in order to ensure that the company's promotions were effective.

The first activity on the list was to make closer contact with customers, and to involve them in the decision-making over new products and service arrangements. This was a far more direct way of gauging information than using consultants as intermediaries, as they had done before.

In another company, I had the opportunity to accompany salesmen involved in the merchandising of wines and beers. One particular representative had a close understanding of his client's business. His visits to take orders and update the client on the latest developments took place approximately every 10 days. During these visits, the representative also gave advice on merchandising schemes. He was not just selling, but helping through sound advice based on his knowledge of the trade. It was clear that the close links he maintained were the key to success in addition to his promotional work.

Integrated promotion

Often a team's promotional activity is not considered an integral part of the operation. For example, advertising has often been contracted out to specific agencies. In some companies, the Promoting is done on an arm's-length basis via leaflets through the post, or through adverts in newspapers or on television. However, where products involve regular understanding of customer needs it is vital to develop a close relationship with the users and for all team members to realize that they have a role to play in promotion.

Today, for example, many companies use focus groups to gauge what their customers think of their products. Others set up specific events, such as 'open days', where they can interact with their customers and give them a clearer understanding of what they are doing. It is vital for people in the manufacturing and the servicing aspect of the work to understand their role in promotion. This is particularly so for those companies that have physical deliveries. In such cases, the client organization members see more of the delivery drivers than anyone else from the supplier.

Summary

Promoting needs to become an integral part of the way your team works in order to produce more effective results. Here are several questions you can ask your team:

- Who are our clients?
- What impression do they have of us?
- How can we communicate effectively with them on a regular basis?
- What issues should we address with them?
- How can we establish a 'promotions' plan for all of our clients, both internal and external?
- Which media should we use to promote?

Be wary of assigning the Promoting function to an individual, or an external group such as an advertising agency, and then forgetting about it. Successful teams integrate it in all their activities, no matter what the major focus of their work is.

Also, remember that internal Promotion is as important as external Promotion. This is often overlooked, but it is essential that each unit in an organization communicates with other units as if they were external clients, and gives the right impression all of the time.

All promotion, negative or positive, has an impact internally and externally. As illustrated, negative promotion can have even more of an impact than positive promotion. Words as much as deeds can turn the attitudes of people for or against very quickly. All team members should be trained in the impact of negative and positive promotion.

It is very important to concentrate on the Promoting function throughout the allocation of special time to discuss the way it is being done. The objective is usually to strengthen links with customers and colleagues, but does it work that way? Do not take it for granted. Remember the old saying: 'If you don't look after your customers, someone else will'.

EXERCISE
- What does Promoting mean in your work?
- How can you and your team improve internal and external Promoting work?

CHAPTER SIX

Developing work – ways to test and plan

Preparing the ground

In each organization a lot of work goes on before products are sold or services delivered. The success of the products and services depends substantially on how well people do what we call the Developing work. That work covers the many aspects of planning and preparation. It is an important area of teamwork. These activities include:

- market testing of a new product
- developing and improving an existing product
- analyzing the facts and figures relating to a new acquisition
- helping introduce a new service
- developing a budget
- planning at all levels, particularly for contingencies
- developing new business
- providing better access to markets
- working on the reorganization of business facilities
- arranging to turn concepts into realities
- developing new operational systems.

In our work with teams, we have found many of them performing well in the areas of Advising, Innovating and Promoting. However, they do not always perform as effectively as they should in the area of Developing. Too often, there is a gap between a good idea and its application. For example, an idea may have been well researched, but insufficiently developed as a product or service for the market.

Developing work is the area between operating the existing business and introducing improvements to products and services. It is the area that deals with the middle ground of transforming 'what is' to 'what could be' and 'what will be'. It is a vital area for any team and any business.

John Herschell, Marketing Manager for a detergent company, with whom I worked, said, 'People can have the right information, good ideas, and even promote what they do, but unless they develop their products or services to suit their customers' needs, they will not be successful'.

Skills used in Developing work

Those who particularly enjoy Developing kinds of work like to use their analytical and logical skills and abilities. They will listen to an opinion, but in the end put the major emphasis on facts and figures. They like to test things. They are very analytical. They are not satisfied until they understand as objectively as possible how people will view the product, service or project under development. By doing this, they are able to stand back from the ideas and the beliefs and assess things.

CASE STUDY

A product manager for a women's clothing company told me:

I spend most of my time at work in a development role. Being in the fashion industry we see many changes. My job is to assess what the changes are, and help develop new products, so that we are always up to date.

I am often involved in projects. I meet with various groups of women who form our focus group discussion panels. We show them the ideas. It is my job to listen to their views and assess them, so that we can come up with something successful.

It's a challenging job because I have to take people's opinions and see what is feasible on a day-to-day basis. I also have to communicate with our designers, and our dress-makers, expressing exactly what is required, and finally test those ideas in the marketplace.

Assessing opportunities

A key part of any Development activity is to see, in advance, how a new idea can be made to work. The basic research may have been done. The testing and experimentation may have been done, and the finance raised. In addition, the system to make the product or service work on a regular basis needs to be developed. It requires someone who has good Linking skills, as well as the analytical and practical experience to make things work.

Eric Pinder is involved in Developing work. He works for a publishing company, and concentrates on acquisitions. He described his work:

> Each day, I receive a number of telephone calls and letters indicating that certain publications are available for sale. Each one of them is an opportunity that has to be followed up on a project basis. My job is to assess which of the opportunities are likely to succeed. I do this in various stages. The first is a financial analysis on the figures that are provided.
>
> The next most important step is to visit the people who are selling the publications, and discuss with them in detail the history and content of the product. These two steps help me decide whether we could make a success of it.
>
> Many people are involved in our organization. Some of them promote existing publications, others produce the publications, and others write the material, or give advice on how we can keep up with new opportunities.
>
> I must Link both internally and externally with them to assess and develop the publication on offer. Then, I find a way to ensure it fits in with the existing facilities for production and promotion.

Those who are successfully involved in Developing work recognize how important it is to link, and to integrate with the work of other team members. On one of my consulting assignments with a major airline, I asked a flight captain what work he did when he was not flying. He replied,

> I have an interesting project-management role, that involves sitting on a committee that plans the introduction of new aircraft. At least once a year, with our team, I visit the Boeing company, to assess what they have to offer. We give the specifications on what our corporation requires. It's an interesting part of my job, as it means I'm involved in the planning of new operations.

As with all work functions, these are examples of the internal and the external aspects of Developing. The main focus on the external aspects comes from the interaction with the customers and competitors. It is vital to have people who are Linking externally, to ensure you are up to date. Likewise, it is important to focus on the internal Linking aspects, which usually relate to the planning and establishing of new ways of operating. Both of these aspects will be reflected in the seven key areas of Developing.

The seven main areas

Developing work can be studied in the following seven areas: business development, technical development, product development, service development, market development and, on the human resources side, personal and team development. All of these are interlinked, but in practice we often plan one area without reference to the others. An overview of these areas and the Linking aspects is given below.

Business development

This area is crucial to any company and any team. It is normal to have an annual business plan, but many organizations review this quarterly against fast-emerging trends and changes. The business development plan should subsume all the other aspects of development, but be led by the demands of the customer. Therefore, business plans will only be as good as the external assessment and external Linking that has gone to make that assessment.

Technical development

Technical development usually means research on products, but it also covers technical issues like safety and security. Most organizations have plans for activities in this area, but the speed of change is catching a lot of organizations out. The cost of technical investment as a proportion of sales can rise, thereby reducing profits. External Linking is essential if the organization is to keep up to date. Increasingly, this creates major alliances between companies, who previously felt they could go it alone.

Product development

Those organizations that have very successful products are often poor at product development, because they have got used to relying on the one successful product. There are of course overlaps between technical development and product development, but the two areas are different. The first looks at technology, and all aspects of the technical infra-structure. However, there needs to be a separate product development plan. The classic example of one that went wrong is that of Coca Cola. After having a successful formula for the product of their leading drink, which lasted for decades, they decided to change it. Despite much testing and market-research work, they got it wrong. Customers rebelled. The company was forced to return to the previous version.

Service development

This is increasingly the big difference between one company and another. Today, most companies have the same technology. The major mark of distinction is the level of administrative and personal service. It is here that the interpersonal skills, as well as the administrative systems, have to be first class. It is again an example of where the role of Linking comes to the fore, particularly when a staff member, rather than just fulfilling an order, makes the effort to give helpful advice. It is not just a friendly voice at the end of the telephone, although that is important. It is the thinking, caring, person who makes the right links to provide the service. That is often a lorry driver. No longer are they just drivers and distributors, they are key Linkers with the customer and integral to the service provided. Yet, unfortunately they are not always treated that way, nor trained as Linkers.

Marketing development

This is recognized by most companies as important, if measured by the amount of money they put behind market-research efforts to gain market share. Indeed, considerable efforts are made to develop new markets, not only through advertising but by widening the appeal of the products to different age groups. Marketing has become a science in its own right through the various techniques that have been created. Therefore, in any consideration of the application of the Developing work function its role in marketing has to be high on the list.

Team development

This has become a major feature of successful organizations. It is no longer assumed that if everyone does their job well the total sum of the parts will provide effective teamwork. Team supervisors and leaders are asked to develop their teams, not just allocate work. They are required to be Linkers, and be proficient in all the eleven skills. Team development is now a skill required of all managers, albeit that some of them who have not acquired Linking skills find it very difficult.

Personal development

Large organizations, until relatively recently, provided reasonable guarantees of employment to their professional staff, and with it career development. These assumptions are no longer valid. With the new situation comes the obligation for each individual to look after their personal career development.

CASE STUDY: SELF DEVELOPMENT

When we discuss the issue of development with individuals, they all agree that they need to spend time developing themselves. It is particularly important for those who have to keep up to date with professional advances.

In one of our meetings, Susan Bayes, an accountant, stated:

The professional field in which I work is moving so quickly that it is important to allocate at least 10 per cent of my time to keeping up to date. I do this through reading, attending workshops and conferences, and also getting involved with the professional association.

This kind of personal development is vital. We have recently set up a local group of accountants who meet on specific topics to look at what we should be doing to improve our knowledge. Personally, I find it very useful. It helps me keep up to date with the latest software, not to mention the new ideas that are coming through, in terms of the technical aspects of accounting.

The self-development approach is one that we have found to be widespread among other professionals too, such as lawyers, doctors and dentists. The whole issue of Developing is a crucial area in terms of the way in which they manage their careers, and how this contributes to the work of their teams.

Work skills in the Developing area

Developing is an aspect of teamwork essential for any team. Those who enjoy this type of work invariably like going out and meeting with others to talk through what can be done in a practical way to improve things. They are also excellent at bringing a logical and analytical view to what can be done. Rather than just staying with an idea, they want to see it formed into something that can be used. In that sense, they take a pragmatic approach, making links through a project-based approach.

Many of the people who enjoy Developing work get closely involved with the administrative aspects of teamwork. This involves setting up meetings, writing budgets, generating prototypes, arranging for the testing of new ideas, and generally facilitating the movement of innovations into practice. They do not do all of these things themselves, but they do link closely with those who have other specific skills.

Some of them also like to get involved with the Organizing aspect of teamwork, particularly if they are good at arranging the availability of resources. If so, they get involved in setting up timetables and schedules for the operation.

They are people who want to move ideas and innovations forward. They like projects. Involve them where there are new developments.

How to work with Developers

There are two types. One of them, the pragmatic type, has a practical 'hands-on' approach. The other, the creative type, works more with the overall ideas.

Both have an extroverted approach to relationships, and they are therefore outgoing and make contacts easily. They also both have an analytical way of looking at problems, and apply hard logic to any decision. In other respects, they are different.

The pragmatic type:

- has a structured way of working, where order and systems are preferred
- can be very practical in the way they tackle problems.

The pragmatic type also:

- likes to gain a lot of information and examples of things that will work
- will have views based on experience
- will in the main work with what you have, so make sure that it is well prepared.

The creative type, while being extroverted and analytical, has a more flexible and practical approach. The extroverted creative analytical and structured person, in contrast, will look for projects that:

- enable him or her to add an extra dimension
- have a strong focus on the market needs
- use their ideas and plans
- require a well-organized system for action.

Do not go before them half prepared. Make sure that you have your facts and a clear presentation, with a logical order of what should be done.

Developing questions

Overall, the Developing process ensures that all ideas, innovations and market opportunities are fully assessed, so that practical plans can be developed for implementation. It may therefore involve conducting low cost trials and experiments in order to check assumptions and proposals. Key questions to ask when developing new ideas, proposals or projects are:

- How do we ensure that the market and the key stakeholders will accept our ideas?
- What should we do to establish a system that works on a regular basis to deliver the product or service?
- What are the alternatives to our current ways of working?
- How are our competitors changing their operations?

Tests, trials, prototypes, client or customer consultation, and market research are essential for effective Developing. This is what Developers excel at.

To improve your own skills in this area, it is vital to have a questioning attitude. It is worthwhile taking five minutes to jot down the key questions that relate to your team and business over next 12 months. That will help focus where your efforts need to be in all areas of the Team Wheel.

How to focus on Developing

The Developing function is an integral aspect of your meetings and crucial to teamwork. Many people use the Team Wheel as a checklist to ensure that all aspects of the project are covered. It is useful, therefore, to ask team members what they feel is required in order to develop existing products, procedures and services into even better ones.

The process of Developing should apply to all the other work functions in order for improvements to be made. You can ask, for example, how the Promoting, Organizing, and Producing and all the other aspects of the team's work can be developed and improved.

In addition, ask them what they think should be done to develop further teamwork itself. This is one of the most interesting aspects of the Developing function. It covers not only the hard tangible products that a team works on, but also the way the team itself is working. Some of the most interesting discussions with team members have been on assessing what the team needs to do in order to develop itself.

CASE STUDY

In one of my consulting meetings, the team leader summed up various ideas that were suggested as follows:

> It seems that in order to develop ourselves we need to spend more time reviewing our mode of operation, and provide more time for individuals to keep up to date. We should therefore establish a self-development project, where each member can assist one another.

This led to some valuable work on how the team members could develop both the task aspects of their job, and also themselves to meet new challenges. They met in trios to share and compare ideas, and to help each other assess their respective work. As a result, teamwork links improved and overall performance increased.

Guidelines for development

For the business as a whole, as well as the team, the following steps are useful when considering Developing activities:

- gather views on what is required from customers, clients and other key stakeholders
- set objectives on issues and tasks that need development
- generate a plan
- assess the options
- feed these back to the stakeholders and gather their views
- incorporate stakeholders' views and refine the plan
- choose a line of action
- implement the plan
- continue developing the product or service so that it constantly meets your clients' needs.

Summary

This chapter has looked at the role of Developing as a work function in a business, in a team and in a project. The importance of this area is increasing with the speed of change. Any organization, or team, that wants to keep up to date has to put more time and effort and money into it.

As indicated, there are seven main activities in which that effort needs to be concentrated:

- business development
- technical development
- product development
- service development
- market development
- team development
- personal development.

Each of these is interlinked. Therefore, any manager, supervisor, or team leader needs to focus on each one through team discussion, but do so in a way that ensures maximum Linking. One way to do that is to look at the other work functions and have the team review how well the individual members, and the team as a whole, are Linking with each other to Advise, Innovate, Promote, Organize, Produce, Inspect and Maintain the relevant activities.

Developing work is at the heart of the future for any business, team, project or individual. It is worth a lot of thought, time and investment.

EXERCISE

- How effective is your team on the various areas mentioned in this chapter?
- What do you need to do to improve your own personal development?

CHAPTER SEVEN

Organizing work – arranging who does what

Arranging who does what and when

When asked to define management, many people say it is about arranging and organizing people and tasks. However, Organizing, as indicated, is only one of the work functions necessary for success. In this chapter, we look at some of the key points.

The Organizing function is crucial in all aspects of project management. The essence of a team project is that there is a task, not always clearly defined, a time within which it is to be done, and certain resources which can be used. That kind of situation calls for people who can work to objectives, set priorities and cut through the problems to a solution.

It can be exciting, high-energy effort, racing towards a deadline, the adrenaline pushing you on, often to work beyond normal time. It is work in which you can see a result in a relatively short time, if you can get people working in the right direction.

It may be surprising that Organizing is often one of the key areas of teamwork that creates problems. Firstly, people do not always enjoy being organized by others, particularly those who are in a temporary project leader role. Secondly, there are often different viewpoints of what kind of organizational arrangements are necessary. Therefore, this function is often one of the most contentious issues in teamwork.

CASE STUDY

In the oil-refining business, it is normal to have a number of project teams working on various assignments. One of the companies in which I was consulting had problems because the project teams did not work together well. I introduced them to the Team Management Wheel to assess where the problems were.

The Refinery Manager said,

> We have people who are technically knowledgeable to do the job. However, they do not complete the projects on time and budget because they argue over the organizational issues. Although we have project leaders appointed, they do not have the same loyalty and acceptance as the departmental managers.
>
> You have to be particularly good at bringing people together. That starts with being organized yourself before you organize others. We have noticed that many of the meetings can end up as shouting matches unless the project manager is an effective chairperson. We have therefore started to give the project managers more training in that aspect of their role.

Organizing services

Each day in your own job you will no doubt be involved in many Organizing activities. These can range from establishing an appointment, or meeting someone, to indicating to a colleague what you want them to do. It is particularly important if you are in a support role. Here, you are providing the pitch upon which others will play. Although you have the authority within your own team, you are probably seen by the client as their project manager, as shown below.

Pat Johnson, an administrative manager with one of the training companies with which we worked, talked about the work she does.

> In my job I spend most of my time organizing procedures, particularly making arrangements for visitors. We also ensure that the various resources are available for people to do their work, from the time they arrive to departure including the leisure facilities. It sounds easy, but in practice we are often under pressure because the arrangements change at the last moment, for example, when more people turn up than was planned, or there is a cancellation. On such occasions, we have problems, as everyone wants priority.

Tools for Organizing

We are increasingly offered Organizing tools. At the simplest level, you may only need to jot down times and activities in a diary. Maybe you have invested in an electronic organizer, or mobile telephone that integrates such services into its functions.

At a different level, on projects, you may need to use such aids as Gantt Charts, or programme evaluation and review techniques. In addition, there are statistical techniques that can help you to plan scheduling of tasks, to ensure that the various activities of your overall project are scheduled. And, with the advent of computers, many of the complex Organizing activities can now be done electronically through project management software.

Organizing before the project

The best team projects are those in which considerable preparation has been done before the project itself starts. As a team leader, it is important to negotiate that planning time. It will save a multitude of problems later. The techniques and software systems available certainly make the thinking and understanding easier once you have grasped the main ideas. They can show the shortest time to conduct a project and the best schedule. They can indicate the best order for arranging the supply of materials and when they should be delivered.

CASE STUDY

Peter Dixon is a builder who built a house for me. His main role is to organize the provision of people and materials to ensure that a housing development is completed on time. He said,

> Team management, for me, is mainly project management. I have to get all the people and materials in the right place to ensure the job can be done. I spend a lot of my time identifying the order for the work to be done, then finding the right people, and ensuring that they have the resources to do the job.
>
> The people who work for me are well trained. They know how to build a house, but the difficult aspect of my job is in organizing the project before we get to the building site. It involves an enormous amount of negotiation and planning. We have to be sure that, when we start to build, all the plans and the materials are in place, before we start the on-site operations.

Four key areas of Organizing

Therefore, let us look at various aspects of Organizing. There are four main dimensions that require consideration in Organizing, and they are interlinked as shown in the model below.

	Technical	People
Internal	Systems	Staff
External	Contracts	Clients

The Margerison four-factor project management model

The team leader has to allocate time to each area, and to balance one against the other. That is why they have to be excellent Linkers. The job continually demands an analysis of the technical and the human issues, both inside and outside the team organization structure.

Internal technical issues
Most managers I have met say that they feel most at ease with the internal technical issues. After all, that is what their basic training gives them. It may be dealing with accounting systems, or machinery for an oil refinery, or coping with a computer system. The other three areas are often less defined in terms of the specific requirements, and may change as the project develops.

Internal staff issues
Organizing and motivating staff on a project can be difficult, particularly if they are only working on a part-time basis, with their main job somewhere else in the organization. That is why being effective at the team development Linking skill is crucial.

In managing the staff of a team, it is a good rule to 'put personal process before task content'. That means understanding the thoughts and concerns of the people involved before racing too far ahead with the requirements of the task plan. There needs to be a balance. One without the other does not work.

Indeed, put the letters 'P' and 'T' in front of you, to remind you what you are focussing upon. 'P' equals process mode, in which you focus on the arrangements rather than the content of what is said. 'T' equals technical, for the content and the detail relating to a task.

If you sense problems with motivation, quickly move in to 'P' mode. As a Linker, call a meeting to listen, problem-solve and counsel:

easier said than done, but vital to success. Also, if you sense a problem with the system, then focus on 'T', and start asking questions.

External contract issues

Every project has a client or stakeholders. There should always be a contract. If it is with another organization this will invariably be written down as a legal agreement, or as a binding letter. If the client is within your organization, they are still external to the project, and some agreement in writing should be gained. This involves negotiation skills. This is vital to any Organizing work. It is part of interface management Linking skills. A project is usually only as good as the external contract, because from that comes the objectives, the work allocation, the quality standards, the plans and the action.

External client issues

I have been surprised how often team leaders and project managers do not know who the external clients are. They may know the person who set the project in motion, but they do not know the people who will decide if the work will be deemed appropriate. It is always important to find out who the real clients are. Invariably, they are the people who can make, or break, a project.

At the beginning of any project, make sure that they are consulted, and 'sign off' on any agreements. It is best, if possible, to have them on a project committee that meets regularly to review progress. This process helps resolve many problems before they get too large. Relating with, and organizing, external clients is a major Linking skill of a project manager.

How well organized is your team?

When I work with project teams, they often identify Organizing as the key priority for improvement. I start by asking them to make two lists:

- of areas in which they think they are well organized
- of areas in which they feel they need improvement.

The latter is invariably longer than the former.

Usually, the team focusses on the second list, and discusses what kind of organizational arrangements would help improve their performance. One of the issues that frequently comes up for discussion is how to establish clear objectives. This is a major part of action, as everything stems from clarity and agreement on the objectives.

As guidelines on how to organize, the following are very important.

Objectives

- What are your team's objectives?
- Do each of the team members know their own objectives in contributing to the team effort?

It is difficult to get organized if you do not have objectives, or if there is conflict about priorities among team members. Many teams are not clear on the key objectives that they are trying to pursue. Usually, this is because team members have different priorities, and therefore there are disagreements on where the major thrust of the team should be directed. Such issues need to be brought out into the open if everyone is to 'pull in the same direction'.

Resources

Another question I ask, when reviewing the Organizing function with a team is, 'Do you have the resources necessary to achieve the agreed objectives?' These resources may be as diverse as money, people, time, or, in fact, anything that they consider important. I then ask the team to list their resources, and discuss whether or not they are adequate. If not, I ask them to discuss ways in which they can improve the situation.

Roles

There is often a tendency to rush into the task action before getting the work allocation clarified. If this happens, it is usually a case of task before process.

Does your team have clear guidance and understanding of their roles? The Team Wheel is invaluable as a checklist when discussing roles. Having it available, and visually displayed, will facilitate the discussion enormously. I have done this many times. It provides real clarity on who needs to do what, and when, to achieve the results: simple things like discussing what advice and information is required. That leads to the Linking issues of who will be contacted and involved. Likewise, the issues of Innovating, Promoting, Developing and the rest can all be discussed openly using the model as a framework. It works because it is the language of everyday businesses, and the language of teamwork.

Team Co-operation

The essence of good organization is that team members work well together. In short, good Linking leads to effective Organizing. They go together hand-in-glove.

CASE STUDY

In a meeting with a manufacturing team, there was considerable discussion among the team members about the way everything seemed to be rushed. As one person said,

> The problem is that as soon as somebody thinks of an idea they want it implemented! They forget we have to organize things in a proper manner. They want to move from idea to action before they've even organized people and resources. That's why we're having this discussion, and why we've got problems.

As the meeting continued, it became clear that it wasn't just their team experiencing organizational problems. Indeed, many of the issues that they were dealing with stemmed from other disorganized teams that passed their problems down the line.

This is a case for inter-team Linking. If your team is having its work disrupted, or slowed down, because other teams are not organized, it is your job as project manager, or team member, to do something about it. This is a key external Linking role.

Organizing the dialogue

How you present the issues is important. The natural inclination is often to blame the other team. Maybe they are in the wrong. Maybe they are not. However, the way to proceed is to collect the facts, particularly those that affect the working of your team. Then organize a meeting with a person from the other team who can have influence, and get action.

Rather than allocate blame, lay the facts on the table. Say how the situation is affecting your team. Indicate your feelings about the situation. Ask for the views of the other person or people. Outline what you would like to happen. Discuss the matter in true Linking style, by active listening, problem-solving and seeking a mutually beneficial agreement. It is all part of the essential negotiation skills of a Linker who seeks to improve organizational arrangements. This is an essential part of team Linking.

Organizing inter-team Linking

CASE STUDY

In one assignment, two teams had to work together, but problems arose because they were housed in two separate buildings, three miles apart. Customers received conflicting messages about credit allowances from both teams. One team, trying to sell more, offered extended credit terms. The other team, trying to control debts, sent threatening letters if bills were not paid quickly. Needless to say, customers perceived the company as disorganized, even though both teams felt that they were clear on their roles.

When I asked if the issues were ever discussed, I was told that each day messages were sent and phone calls made. However, when I asked when had the two teams last met, the answer was 'never'.

It is hard to believe, but true. I set up a special inter-team event, and within half a day the players had got to know each other and worked out ways of resolving their differences. Personal Linking made the difference in this particular situation – not phone calls or electronic messages.

Organizing yourself

Although the team may be getting its act together, how well do you feel you organize your own time and resources? The mark of an effective team member is the added value they contribute to the team, and this can only be done if everyone is personally well organized.

Your time

The starting-point is invariably in the use of your own time. Once you have established the agreed team objectives, you should assess your own personal objectives, which need to be congruent with the team's. From these, you can allocate your time accordingly. Your own objectives should also contain 'benchmarks', so that you know whether they are being achieved at satisfactory levels of quality.

Your plan

Everyone should also share their personal plan with other team members. Discuss what you plan to do, when you will do it, how you will do it, and indicate the schedule to which you will be working. This discussion is a form of negotiation, enabling each member to make commitments, and to get the agreement of other team members in advance.

Your contribution

A key aspect is personal contributions. At team meetings, get people to focus on what they have contributed, and what they will contribute. In particular, ask them to summarize the organizational commitments into which they are entering. At one meeting a participants said,

> I'm not a particularly well-organized person, but I welcome the opportunity to share what I would do, and how I can improve. It helps me focus, not only my own priorities, but also on what others feel that I should do to help the team.

This kind of activity provides the basis for commitment, as people do not like to fail in what they have promised to. Moreover, it provides a framework in which people can help each other. Each member of the team should act as a Linker to help others.

Working with Organizers

Some people have a natural penchant for Organizing. It is their preferred way of working. Our research shows that there are two types of organizer, which I will call 'A' and 'B'.

Type A are the more extroverted type. They like to make up their mind quickly on what to do and get on with the action. They talk more than others to get their point across. They are often forceful in negotiating and bargaining. The more mature type A person comes across as self-assured. The less mature come across as bombastic and arrogant. A type Organizers invariably have their eyes and mind on the main points. They are practical in their approach, and set specific objectives. They then apply any tool or technique that will help them analyze the situation, and come to a conclusion. Once they have made a decision, they implement it with enormous energy, until the system is working.

So in working with these kinds of people, make sure that you know your facts, know your rights, know what you want and be prepared to argue your case. The extroverted Organizer type is a person of action. Do not be surprised if they get on with the job, sometimes before you feel proper agreements have been made. Indeed, you need to make sure that proper processes are put in place, with agendas for meetings, paperwork prepared in advance and read. After the meeting, make sure the notes signed off. That is good practice anyway, but essential when you are working with those that have a high Organizing preference.

Type B Organizers have a quieter disposition, and organize in a different way. They are usually quite creative, and dream up ideas that they would like to see operating. They apply a logical reasoning approach to problem-solving and, when convinced, get into action. However, because they are more inclined to work by themselves in the planning phase, it is likely that colleagues and staff are not always privy to their thinking. Colleagues can be surprised when they are confronted with deadlines and plans.

This kind of Organizer should call meetings and involve people, though that is not their natural way of doing things. They like to have everything sorted out before they tell others. It can come across as a *fait accompli*, rather than a discussion.

So if you are working with this kind of person, ask them what they are doing and help them become better at communicating their ideas.

Organizing guidelines

Organizing involves establishing key business objectives and then managing day-to-day events to achieve them by setting deadlines, conducting meetings, co-ordinating activities and deciding priorities. A checklist that can be useful for project team discussions is as follows.

- What are our objectives?
- When should we achieve them?
- Who will do what?
- What resources do we need in order to do the job?
- If problems occur, how will we get back on track?
- What are the immediate priorities?

Focussing on these questions will improve your team's Organizing function, and help each member to become more effective at project Linking. This chapter has outlined the way Organizing is part of the total process of team management.

EXERCISE

- Look at the team projects in which you have been involved, and note the learning points that you have gained on how to be more effective at Organizing?
- What must you do to become more organized?

CHAPTER EIGHT

Producing work – ways of delivering results

Producing the goods

The sharp end of any teamwork is production of products and service delivery. The customer judges the results of teamwork by your outputs. Using the language of our team model, the customer needs to be impressed with:

- the quality of advice they get
- the innovation they see
- the power of your promotion
- the depth of development work
- the efficiency of the organization
- the attention to inspecting details
- the standards of maintenance care.

However, all those will be of secondary concern if the product or service is not up to expectations.

When I refer to Producing, that includes the production of services, such as those you get in a restaurant, bank or post office. Also included are the delivery of products and services, because that is, as far as the customer is concerned, what they are buying. From the customer's viewpoint, for example, the meal at the restaurant is not just what is cooked in the kitchen, but the delivery and service.

Sami Haon, who owns and manages a restaurant, summed it up well.

> We cater for the people who do not want the 'eat it quick', fast food kind of meal. Our clients prefer to have a night out, and take their time to enjoy themselves. However, the principles are the same. We have to deliver high

quality meals and service. In that sense, each meal we produce is a project, and we try to relate with customers on a personal basis to cater for their special needs and tastes.

The customer's view

This chapter will take a customer's view of Producing, because it is the clients who pay, and they judge the results. To them, service and delivery are all part of the end result. This is important when assessing the way in which any project is managed.

By taking a customer's view of Producing, the key issues of external, as well as internal, Linking come into focus. For too long, the production and service roles have been seen as the introverted side of the business, looking inwards rather than outwards.

CASE STUDY

This example is from a meeting of senior managers in a large company with which I was consulting. They were discussing how to meet the needs of the customer more effectively. There was considerable discussion on making closer contact with customers to understand their needs. There seemed to be general agreement on the proposal from those who had spoken. The director in charge of their manufacturing operations, however, had said nothing during the discussion, though he was listening intently.

Eventually, he leaned forward and said,

> It seems that there is a strong view that we should get closer to our customers, and have them get closer to us. However, let's look at what actually happens in practice. The reality is that I have never been invited by our sales people to go and meet a customer at their place of work. And I have to say, I have not taken the initiative to invite customers to see our operations. So we need to change the behaviours, not just the words.

This brought everyone down to earth in terms of the practicalities. It provoked a considerable debate on the current links and those that were required. In particular, the team realized that it needed to look inside before going outside. Team members agreed that stronger internal links between the manufacturing and the sales teams had to be established with joint meetings. This was the first step, the basis for building better and wider external links with customers. The teams realized that they had to break down the silent inside barriers before they could strengthen links with customers.

How Producing work has changed

The people who originally thought up ways of improving production instituted rigorous systems to ensure that everyone knew what they were doing. The aim was to get people working to a fixed plan. In the nineteenth century, during the industrial revolution, many factories set up production systems in which employees worked long hours, doing repetitive work in poor conditions.

By the early twentieth century, people had begun to study the production system. Frederick Taylor achieved fame for introducing 'the scientific method' into business. He studied each person's job, and timed how long it took to do various activities. He broke each job down into components, and rewarded people for the amount that they produced. Initially, this system worked with an uneducated and dependent labour-force with little alternative employment.

Henry Ford developed a production system to mass-produce cars by this method. He set up a 'production line' based on division of labour, which resulted in the manufacture of a greater number of cars in a shorter time and at lower unit cost.

These methods of production, based on dividing work into elemental forms, became the standard way of operating, but there was little, if any, teamwork. Each person did his or her assigned task. They were not involved in work functions such as Advising, Innovating and Promoting. Workers were essentially treated as human machines, and outputs were therefore not optimum.

Today, people are more mobile in searching for work, and most people want to use a range of skills, and have some say in how they work. Productions systems are still an important part of the modern factory, but today there is often more effort to include people in the system design. Productivity improvements can be achieved when people are formed into work-based teams, and empowered to design their own production systems. However, in my experience there is insufficient attention paid to the Linking aspects. It is through the internal and external links that people in the Producing areas can make major contributions with their experience.

Changing patterns

The essential nature of the Producing function has not changed. It involves a systematic and structured way of enabling people to complete jobs on time. The difference is that those producing this work can now be part of front-line service. A prime example of an established, standardized production system is the 'fast food' outlet.

The McDonald's chain of hamburger restaurants produces a limited menu of food quickly and efficiently. No matter where you are in the world, you can visit a McDonald's restaurant and expect the same level of service. This level can only be achieved, however, by adhering to the production system, regardless of culture or place. It requires great administrative Linking to ensure that good teamwork meets those standards.

It also shows how Producing work can link up with Promoting work. The people in the front line are representing the company and putting out its message.

Once people are clear about what they have to do, and have quality systems to follow, they will know exactly what is expected of them each day. Equally, managers can concentrate on the organization's overall operation, based on its systems, rather than having to solve a different range of problems every day.

Images and activities

Often, the Producing function has been portrayed as less exciting than other areas. It is time to look at this function in a new light, based on the customer's view.

To do this, it is important that those who work in this area become more proactive and see how they can link with the other work functions. Here are some ways in which this can happen.

- Producing and Innovating – whenever possible, there should be an attempt to reduce the space between Innovators who are working in a detached way from those producing the products and services. There needs to be closer involvement of those working on the current and future systems.

- Producing and Organizing – there is often a close link between these areas, but sometimes plans are made without the implications being worked through.
- Producing and Promoting – joint meetings need to be set up to help those working in this area work more closely together.
- Producing and Advising – information to and from the Producing function is central to the success of the business. Normally, the cost accountant will be the main internal advisory link on financial matters. However, it is useful to make a full list of the advisory issues that could make the production area more effective. Then, those involved should collect and share the data, rather than having consultants from outside imposed upon them.

Internal and external Linking with the other functions requires time to relate with others, to ask the right questions and assess the responses. If these actions are taken, those involved in Producing will improve their performance.

Innovative production

Work in the Producing area has become a science in its own right. Organizations throughout the world now conduct system studies to see how they can produce their products more quickly and more efficiently. No longer is it just a matter of having an efficient division of labour.

Today, it is a science with a human face. The modern version of Ford, for example, invites and receives millions of suggestions from its staff on how to improve performance. Indeed, Toyota has made this a feature of the employment practice and offers substantial rewards for those whose ideas are adopted. On a wider front, the quality movement has challenged the hard division of labour, advocating involvement in improving the production system.

In a visit to a large food company, I was impressed with how team members were regularly given opportunities to share their ideas with supervisors in special meetings.

In manufacturing plants, instant communication is made available via an intranet. Operatives use computers to feed back information. They can even stop the assembly line, if required, for safety or quality purposes.

In these ways, the nature of the production function is changing. It is focussing more on gaining advice from the people doing the work. It is encouraging more advice and innovation whilst keeping the existing system going. It is helping those in the Producing area get closer to customers. These changes will have a big impact.

Production is a popular work choice

In our research, we have found that about one fifth of the people interviewed enjoyed working in the Producing area, putting it as their first choice of the major areas on the Team Wheel. Typically, they described their preferred way of working as having:

- a practical hands-on approach
- a focus on real tangible problems and projects
- objectives and deadlines
- systematic methods, conforming to a plan
- conscientiousness about meeting deadlines and working to the plan
- a need for a clear structure and an indication of who will do what
- a willingness to do the job in the same way each day, providing that the system works
- a system that runs, rather than one that is continually changed
- neatness and tidiness, with everything in order.

Leadership Linking roles

These preferences have implications for the work of managers or supervisors. Just as considerable change has occurred in organizations, so has change come to the traditional role of the team leader and supervisor. The multi-skilling of the workforce, and allocation of more responsibility, has required a more participative style of management. There has also been a reduction in the number of supervisory levels and, in some cases, 'self-managing' teams have been developed.

As the level of professionalism increases, team members are becoming more involved in the planning and supervision of their own work. This a major shift in teamwork culture from that which existed only a few years ago. Now teams are more involved in discussing objectives and issues. Increasingly, team members are asked to agree on output targets, and to decide amongst themselves how they can be achieved.

All of this supports the Linking concept. It requires that the managers and supervisors see themselves as helping the team members to achieve the targets, rather than directing them to do so. The Linking skills are applicable to all managers and supervisors, but particularly to those in the Producing area, where the outputs are often more visible and deadlines have to be met.

It is often suggested that managers and supervisors need to develop the soft interpersonal skills, but Linking skills in production or any other area are not as soft. A manager or supervisor working effectively as a Linker will be:

- proactive, looking for opportunities for the team
- reactive, quick to pick up concerns and problems
- outgoing, to make contacts that will benefit the team
- receptive to ideas and thoughts from team members
- active, pushing forward with the best ideas to test and implement them.

How to work with Producers

People who enjoy working in the Producing function have preferred ways of operating. There are two main types of Producer.

The A Type, as we shall call them, is more likely to work in the following ways:

- Relationships – they are more introverted than extroverted in preference, willing to work on a task by themselves for concentrated periods of time. They dislike interruptions.
- Work style – they are more practical in emphasis than theoretical. They like to know what the task is and to use tools and techniques, rather than just ideas and concepts.
- Problem-solving – they can be very analytical in a detached kind of way, assessing the evidence in relation to the objectives. After coming to conclusions, they expect them to be implemented without too much discussion, because they provide an efficient solution. They may ignore some of the personal feelings issues in order to get the job done.
- Operational focus – their focus will be to establish a system quickly within which they and others work. The task will be broken down into sequential parts, and each person assigned their part with a deadline and indications of action outputs required. They like to work to a schedule.

The B Type approaches things in the following ways:

- Relationships – they are more extroverted than introverted, and enjoy meeting and discussing issues with others, but usually on a practical 'let's solve the problem' level.
- Work style – they have the same practical interests as type A. They like to get into the detail of how things will work, using tools and techniques, rather than just ideas and concepts.
- Problem-solving – their approach to problem-solving can be different. They start with a strong set of opinions, based on their basic beliefs about the way people should be treated, and what is fair and right. These criteria determine the way in which they will react to the terms and conditions of work. On technical matters, however, they tend to be as logical as anyone when assessing the problems.

■ Operational focus – they have a similar approach to type A in their approach to the operational side of work. They need systems and structures. If these are not there, they will establish them to provide the framework within which they and others work, including defining the roles, procedures and plans.

It is, therefore, useful to understand these points when you are working with such people. It is usually easy to see if a person is more extroverted or introverted, and you can usually find out how strong a person's opinions and values are with a few open questions.

Team work guidelines

When working with people who prefer the Producing side of the business, the following guidelines can be helpful.

■ Take a planned approach to meetings with them.
■ Agree the agendas in advance, and have 'notes of understanding' written up afterwards.
■ Prepare in advance, and read any papers that are circulated, for they will know the details.
■ Be aware of any issues for negotiation, and prepare for those carefully, whether they are within the team, or for and on behalf of the team.
■ Get to the point as soon as possible, as they do not like to waste time.
■ Ensure that any discord or problems are quickly addressed, rather than being allowed to fester.
■ Listen carefully to what they say, and summarize it, so that they know you understand – even if you do not always agree with them.
■ Agree a plan for action, and monitor it, so that everyone gets timely feedback.
■ Let them get into action, and show what they can contribute.

These points are the basis for positive Linking and leadership in situations in which there can be ambiguity and considerable change going on. The modern manager and supervisor, first and foremost, needs to be a Linker, both within the team and for and on behalf of the team. It requires a person who:

■ has a quick mind, willing to listen and discuss issues on their merits
■ is aware of the facts and figures
■ is able to talk to people in a way that helps them understand the issues and focus their efforts on Producing.

Ensuring delivery

In the past, it was sufficient to produce something, store it in the warehouse, and leave it to other people to deliver to the customer. Today, however, the actual delivery of products is increasingly part of the production process. This is where the principles of Producing are carried through to the selling arena.

That is why it is important to see the production of products and services from the customer's point of view. Modern retailing is a good example of the production-delivery process. When you shop at a major retail store, such as Marks & Spencer, you will notice that the layout is neat, tidy, and systematic. Likewise, if you visit your local music store, you will notice CDs and tapes laid out in neat rows, suitably labelled and clearly marked. Organized production methods are part of the promotion and selling process.

The more we move toward 'just-in-time' delivery, the more producing, promoting and selling need to work to one well-organized system.

Summary

Any team can generate information, come up with good ideas, and go out and promote what it has, but unless it actually produces according to the customer's specifications, all efforts are wasted.

Improvement in production and service delivery needs to start with a review of all the internal and external links with a view to satisfying customer needs. Project management has a major part to play in this by involving people in task forces to look at the key issues and how to improve things. The Producing function depends on regular reviews of the operational systems and the establishment of newer, more efficient, systems to replace older ones.

Here are some guidelines that may be helpful:

- Involve all team members in discussions about the current production system.
- Define what your products or services are. Use an obvious question like 'what do we mean by production?'
- List who are the customers and clients for what you produce, and who links with them – the last bit is crucial, and you are likely to find some gaps.
- Draw up a process flowsheet of the production process, from the moment the order arrives from the client or customer, right through

to final delivery. Check if it actually works like that in practice. Again, it will be surprising if you do not find some gaps.

- Talk with customers and clients, and hear what they say about your service, and what links they think are needed to improve things.
- Become a customer of your own organization and find out what service you get.

These guidelines are the basis for reviewing the production process and the formation of project groups. They sound simple. In practice, they are much talked about, but when the actual situation is assessed there are many gaps and issues to be worked on.

EXERCISE

- What do you personally produce?
- With whom do you need to meet to share information and ideas on how your team could be more effective in the Producing area?

CHAPTER NINE

Inspecting work – how to get the details right

Perceptions of Inspecting

Inspecting is an activity often underrated by teams. It is sometimes seen as adding to costs, rather than producing the product or service. Also, it is regarded more as a negative activity than a positive one.

However, when things go wrong, it is usually because a team has not completed the Inspecting activity as well as it should have. It is called 'human error', in contrast to mechanical error. That is, the disaster could have been avoided.

Catastrophes

In two catastrophic incidents, namely the Chernobyl nuclear explosion and the Bhopal chemical disaster in India, the lack of Inspecting created untold misery, suffering and death. At Chernobyl, the staff did not follow the procedures. At Bhopal, despite warnings, the problems that caused the disaster were not attended to.

Both disasters attracted huge media attention, and they highlighted the consequences of not following established processes and safety procedures. Disasters of this magnitude show the necessity of having a first-class Inspecting function.

Day-to-day Inspecting work

The Inspecting function is of paramount importance every day. Each activity involves attention to detail. It may be a plumber fitting a new drain or an electrician putting in a new wire.

It is essential to finalize any business deal with a contract. These important documents are there to govern who gets what and to avoid later disagreements. However, many business dealings end up in court over disputes because the necessary Inspecting procedures were not put in place.

We are all subject to Inspecting activity. Perhaps the most prevalent is submitting our annual tax returns, and complying with the tax inspector's rules and regulations. We also encounter inspection on more pleasurable activities, such as travel.

Inspecting in the travel industry

The travel industry is one in which we encounter many personal inspections. For example, reflect on any holiday or business trip when you travel by plane. Here are just a few of the inspections you can expect en route, before you get on the plane.

- You arrive at the airport car park, take a ticket and place it in a safe place for the check-out inspection when you leave.
- You go to the airport check-in desk, and present your ticket for inspection.
- You then have your bags checked via the X-ray machine, and answer the security questions.
- You go through the metal detector to see if you are carrying any suspect materials.
- A security person may give you a 'body check'.
- If you are travelling abroad, you have to present your passport for a check.
- There may be another security check of any hand luggage.
- You go to the gate for your flight, and have your boarding card checked before getting on the plane.

You have been involved in eight or more acts of Inspecting already, and you have not even begun the flight.

Ruth Swanson, who works for a security company at an airport, said,

People seem to accept our role, but dislike being searched. However, I think they recognize that our inspections ensure everyone's safety.

My colleagues and myself are trained to work as a team, so that one of us is looking at luggage while others are doing personal searches. It is very important that we are able to communicate quickly, and let each other know when we see something unusual.

On arrival at your destination airport, there are more checks.

- Customs control on the red gate will check any items, and even if you go through the green area you may be checked.

- Immigration will want to check your passport and return ticket, and maybe your visa.
- Security officers may want to check your bags, and some have dogs that sniff your bags for illegal substances, such as drugs.

However, it is not just the ordinary passengers who may be carrying banned substances, or dangerous weapons that the customs and immigrations services are looking for. Organized criminals cross international borders.

A manager in the customs service said:

We have had to change the way we work so that we can deal with the increasing threats from organized crime. Today, we put far more emphasis on advance detection of those who carry illegal substances. We also have better international links in place, such as task forces in major tourist countries, which means we can now relate more effectively across borders.

The role of Inspecting in the aviation industry, inclusive of customs and other agencies, is a big business in itself. If we look at the money, time and effort put into security, and similar inspecting work in other industries, it is a major employer of people.

It is not only the passengers who are inspected. In addition, a major amount of inspection work is done by those who fly the airplanes.

Welcome on board

For three years, I was involved in the aviation industry. My job was to help the captains and their crew improve teamwork and safety in the cockpit. Our team analyzed closely what captains, co-pilots and flight engineers do, from the time that they enter the airport until they take off in their aircraft.

After checking in to their Mess Room, they go for a briefing on the weather conditions and collect their flight information. After this Advising aspect of their work, they start the Inspecting work.

In most cases, they inherit an aircraft that has flown in from somewhere else, so airworthiness must be checked. The pilots usually walk around the aircraft. They also look underneath the aircraft to conduct a visual check, even kicking the tyres as a rough test of the air pressure on some occasions.

Once inside the cockpit, both the captain and co-pilot go through a set of standard operating procedures (SOPs). This is a checklist of points they need to cover before the flight can be cleared for take-off.

Captain John Walker, one of the pilots, said,

> To me, inspection is a vital aspect of our job. Indeed, we cannot start the flight until we are completely confident the aircraft is in good order. I consider inspection a very positive aspect of our teamwork, and the more people that are involved in it, the better.

Inspection by teamwork

There have been major changes towards the Inspecting function in industry. Until a few years ago, the main emphasis was placed on inspectors to examine products both during and after the production process. If they found any defects, they would refer them back to the production line for improvement or rejection.

Today, the Inspecting function is increasingly integrated into the actual production process. A production manager in a chemical company, where we introduced TMS, told me,

> All team members are involved in inspection, and they are accountable for their own quality. We encourage them to have team meetings whenever they see a problem occurring. Anyone has the right to stop the production line to call a team meeting.

This new approach to Inspecting ensures that the people who are producing an article or service are involved with checking the quality of their work. Rather than seeing this work as a negative activity, it needs to be seen as essential to improve quality.

The costs and returns

But how much should you add to the cost for setting up inspection systems? This is difficult issue. In every industry, people will say that safety and security will not be compromised. Yet at the same time there is a cost for every extra per cent of inspection. Insurance companies spend a lot of time calculating the odds. There will always be accidents, but money put into effective inspection can reduce them.

Many teams are paid on the basis of zero defects, a better way to go than the punishment model. Their rewards and motivation are built around positive Inspecting. But there is more to it than having a good Inspecting function, as the following case shows.

CASE STUDY

I was involved with a subsidiary of a world chemical company assessing ways of improving safety. It was well aware of the costs of inspection, and the costs of the problems. Its insurance bill was incredibly high. It measured itself against Dupont, renowned for its high standard of safety and measures for ensuring high levels of performance. The company with which I was consulting had fallen well below these standards.

There were some managers in the company who felt that penalties and fines would improve performance. There were others who said 'Let's put more money into training'. Other people felt that more investment in advanced technology would reduce safety risks. Above all, the directors and safety committee agreed that continual inspections were essential. All the options were costly, but not as costly as paying higher insurance or having a major accident.

I was asked how teamwork could improve inspections and reduce accident levels. My answer was to start by finding the problems of concern to people in the workplace. I showed the safety committee the Team Wheel. I indicated that teams should be appointed to look at the problem areas of safety in the nine areas of the wheel. We also agreed this would be done on a project approach, rather than classroom training.

FIGURE 9.1: The Margerison McCann Team Wheel

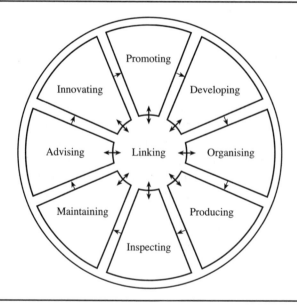

The projects proved that more inspection and tougher penalties were not the answer. The first thing that they discovered was that their Advising function was not good enough. Information of a vital nature was not being exchanged and acted upon because of organizational boundaries. This of course led to an assessment of the Linking between departments, and major gaps were found.

The first projects focussed on life-and-death issues such as fire protection, chemical spillage, transportation of chemicals, site accidents and a host of other points. In each case, by using the Team Wheel the project members and other staff realized where they needed to focus energy. It was not just more checks. It involved getting all of the Team Wheel functions working, and above all Linking between teams throughout the organization. When that started to happen safety rates improved. The head of the safety committee said that it was noticeable that both morale and output increased too.

The customers are right

When we talk to customers, we find that they have a high concern for Inspecting and the quality delivery of the finished product. They want to visit a restaurant and be guaranteed that they will receive a top-quality meal that is safe to eat.

On the retail side, they want assurances that when they buy a camera it works every time. This is one of the reasons that the Japanese moved from bottom of the list to top in only 20 years when it came to selling such products. They focussed on inspection, and raised their quality and reliability.

People want to know for certain that, when they flick the switch on their TV or electric light it will work. In each instance, the product function depends on a high quality of Inspecting.

External Inspecting

This is difficult work. It involves examining the work of others, and keeping them to a standard, which otherwise they may try to avoid. Here are some practical examples.

- Health inspection – to protect the standards of hygiene, governments in most countries have introduced inspectors who have the right to check on restaurants and places where food is sold. This is vital, as we have seen with the outbreak of the dreaded *E. coli* bacteria in meat and the emergence of 'super-bugs' that are increasingly resistant to modern pills and potions.

- Safety inspection – to reduce accidents at work, legislation has been passed in most countries to improve safety at work and the production of safe products. To ensure standards are met, inspectors have the right to check products and places of work, and demand improvements.
- Audit inspection – every business is familiar with the time and the cost of the external auditor who has to certify the financial affairs of the company, and also undertake further in-depth inspections if they are not satisfied. It has become big business, and audit inspections are the basis upon which the major accounting businesses have grown to success and power.
- International inspection – this is, increasingly, becoming more important in an age in which nuclear and chemical weapons can cause devastation. The role of weapons inspectors, as shown in the case of Iraq, where their work was constantly frustrated, is difficult and dangerous. Likewise, we can see similar problems encountered by those who are asked by the UN to inspect and police the brokered peace in the Balkans, or investigate war crimes and human rights abuses.

These are all examples external inspection. The people doing that work have to find the facts, in situations in which their hosts are often trying to hide things. It can be a stressful job. It requires high-level Inspecting skills.

Deliver on the details

I have, however, found situations in which some people actually down-grade Inspecting, saying that it is not an important aspect of their work.

Some advertising people I met on a consulting assignment told me that their main job was creating ideas, not inspecting details. I then met one of their clients, who complained of missed deadlines. I fed this back to the advertising agency.

After analyzing their work, the agency recognized that on a number of occasions they had not delivered the product to the quality required by their customer, or on time. They also realized that they were directing their advertising to people who enjoyed Advising, Innovating, and Promoting work, rather than to people involved in more detailed Inspecting and Maintaining activities. This brought about a discussion on how they could improve their teamwork, to ensure that all activities on the Team Wheel were covered.

They eventually concluded that they needed to put more effort into inspecting and recruiting people who enjoyed that kind of work.

Typically, the people who have a high level of interest in Inspecting and work in an Innovating environment find it difficult, unless they have the support of team members. Therefore it was important that key people in the advertising industry accepted that people focussing on Inspecting work were a valuable part of their business.

Build inspection into teamwork

All functions round the Team Wheel are equally important, and a culture that supports this requires leadership from the top. If this exists, the message will be conveyed and listened to with respect by all team members. For example, those charged with Innovating may get their best ideas from those who are working on the Inspecting functions (as Toyota discovered through its suggestion schemes). Likewise, those charged with Inspecting may get some interesting new approaches by inviting those who are mainly involved in Innovating to contribute to their work.

This is where Linking comes in. However, those who prefer to do the Inspecting kinds of jobs do not always put Linking high on their agenda.

There are many ways in which Inspecting can be built into teamwork. Here are key points that you and your team can ask yourselves, as inspection is initially about the understanding of issues, and only secondly about techniques.

- How do you define Inspecting, in terms of what you do?
- What do you regard as key Inspecting activities in your job?
- Which areas of teamwork demand more Inspecting, and how should it be done?

The answers to these questions can highlight major deficiencies.

CASE STUDY

My son John owns and manages a shop selling diamonds and gold. The main focus every day is on Promoting sales. To expand sales, he introduced a system called 'lay-bys'. This enables a person to deposit 10 per cent on any purchase.

We hold the jewellery for the customer until they have all the money, and the 10 per cent deposit is the basis for that. Often, people also want some alterations done. We do alterations as a separate activity, even on jewellery we have not originally sold ourselves, and these are on the lay-by system.

However, the system led to considerable losses over a period of time. John was doing some inspecting in the business to balance the cash each day, but did not realize a major loss was occurring because of the lay-by system.

When a lay-by item of jewellery was returned to the shop after an alteration it was put into the safe, with the cost of the alteration on it. When the customer came to claim the diamond or gold ring, the staff saw only the price of the alteration, which could be as low as $30–$50. Some of the customers did not tell the sales person the vital information that they owed 90 per cent of the item's price, which could be perhaps $1000 or $2000, in addition to the alteration price.

The person serving the customer was different, in most cases, to the person who made the original sale, Consequently, large sums of money were being lost. It was only when John was personally involved in meeting a customer who came to collect a lay-by that he noticed that only the alteration cost of $30 was on the ticket. He then realized that the inspection and control system was not in place. It was an expensive lesson.

Inspecting and the Team Wheel

One team, with which I worked recognized that it did not have any disaster plan for its business. Its members felt that because they were running a commercial service they could quickly recreate the business. When I asked them about the Inspecting function, they said that some of their business information was on paper and some in computers. The computer data was backed up on a weekly basis, but the paper system had no duplicates.

As a result, the team took it upon themselves to allocate responsibilities for ensuring that audits were done regularly. Also, safety procedures were put in place, so that information could be retrieved should there be any disaster such as fire or robbery.

If you are starting a project to review the function of Inspecting, it can be useful to go round the rest of the Team Wheel and ask the following basic but powerful questions:

- Information advice – what information and advice do we need to improve?

- Innovative ideas – to what extent do we innovate in our approach to Inspecting?
- Promotion work – how well do we promote our Inspecting work?
- Organized action – how well organized are we in our Inspecting work?

These and other questions on the Team Wheel work areas will help identify gaps in your Inspecting work. It will also show where you need to build stronger links.

How to work with Inspector work preferences

Some people really enjoy Inspecting work, and gravitate to it quite happily. Our studies of people who enjoy this kind of work show that there are two types.

Type A Inspectors prefer to work by themselves than with others, but they will contribute clearly and effectively when they feel they know what they are talking about. They should not be rushed. They should be informed in plenty of time what is to be discussed. They will like to consider things carefully. After all, as people who prefer Inspecting, they will want to see if there are any 'holes' in the points.

Those who prefer this kind work have a high need for a practical rather than a theoretical approach. They assess and measure that which they are inspecting, rather than just getting a general feel. They will look for tasks with specific things to do, and the opportunity see if any discrepancies arise.

Some people are attracted to this work because they have strong beliefs about what is right and wrong. In addition, they have a great need for systems and structure. They can therefore be very committed, and at times perhaps obsessive, in the way that they do their work. You need to find out early on what their beliefs are, and see if they are appropriate for the kind of work you plan.

Type B Inspectors are also more introverted in their work relationships. They have a practical emphasis, but they have a different approach to action. They are more laid-back in their approach. They like a lot of evidence before they are convinced, and tend to be seen as sceptical. They see this as a great strength. Because of their need for a lot of data, they may not meet the time deadlines for projects. They also may delay things that they do not like doing, such as meeting those they do not know.

These kinds of people can be exceptional researchers, and gather a wealth of knowledge. However, they do not usually parade or promote this. You need to get to know them well to discover what they know.

They do not always take the time to be proactive Linkers. This can apply both internally and externally. Therefore it is important that they develop and learn the skills of Linking.

Action guidelines

Here are some guidelines to improve your Inspecting processes.

Firstly, discuss with your team whether you need a standard set of operating procedures that everyone can work to. This may cover:

- quality procedures
- financial guidelines
- standard contracts for sales or services
- administration procedures to cover most eventualities.

It is best if the team is involved in the design of these procedures, so that they feel 'ownership', but it is also important to involve experts.

Secondly, it is important to hold regular meetings to assess the information that comes from the Inspecting operations. If the team does not meet to discuss what the data means, no significant improvements will materialize. Remember, the people who do this kind of work are likely to find problems, and may be seen as upsetting progress or slowing things down. Do not be surprised or upset. Inspecting can be a tough job, particularly where you are external to a process.

Thirdly, it is vital for team members to have clear roles in process and procedures. And it is best to choose people who like Inspecting work, rather than assigning the tasks to people who do not enjoy it.

Fourthly, it is important to put in place an audit procedure that ensures that all the processes are reviewed. Too often, procedures are left in place without review, and they become out of date. A 'sunset clause' – to say when a procedure has to be renewed – can be useful as well.

Fifthly, the value of this kind of work should be promoted and made clear to everyone. This is best done through measures that can be seen by all. For example, in factories, wall charts or other visual aids can be installed, so that the number of accidents and the number of safe days or hours that have been worked are clearly seen. In this way, people can measure their achievements, and see how well they are performing.

These steps can be followed as you review quality, finance and accounts, security, safety, contracts and administration procedures. Remember, what gets measured usually gets done.

Summary

This chapter has outlined the positive aspects of Inspecting. It has shown how careful attention to this area can save both lives and money. It can provide a leading edge in an organizations quality and customer service.

Every team needs to set quality standards in this area, and then to establish procedures to check that standards are being met. Look at your own team, and assess how well it does this.

Measuring your success is critical, and benchmarking performance at all levels is essential to progress. Charting techniques go some way towards achieving this, but the approach can be extended to other facets of teamwork. It is more than just having the facts and figures, and controlling the rules and regulations. It requires good Linking with all the other functions, and making Inspecting an integral part of all-round teamwork.

EXERCISE

- What are the main aspects of Inspecting in your job?
- How can you ensure that Inspecting is more integrated into the work of the teams on which you work?

CHAPTER TEN

Maintaining work – ensuring quality support and service

Maintaining standards

A key work function, that can be often underrated is maintenance. There is an old saying that, 'if it is not broken, don't fix it'. This, in some cases, means that maintenance is not done when it should be. When the technology or system does break it is sudden and costly.

In project work, maintenance is often the main reason for the existence of the team. This is particularly so in capital-intensive industries, in which the assessment and repair of equipment on a planned and scheduled basis is essential for continuity of operations.

However, the concept of Maintaining in teamwork has many wider applications. In this chapter, we will look at how you can improve the effectiveness of your team by improving maintenance work at various levels.

Maintaining questions

In discussions with team members, I have asked them what they regard as some of the important issues in the Maintaining area. These are the issues that emerged:

- How do we maintain good relationships with other teams on which we depend?
- How do we maintain quality and productivity?
- How can we ensure good working conditions for staff?
- How do we maintain the trust and confidence of our customers?
- What are the ethical guidelines that govern our work?
- How do we establish a common purpose that holds us all together ?

Why not conduct a special meeting with your own team on these questions and issues? The discussion may generate some emotion. The topics usually involve people's feelings, values and principles, particularly if things are not working as they should. Be prepared for that, and encourage members to listen and respect others' views.

The objective in such meetings is to improve teamwork, not just follow a particular member's own obsession. All members need to feel free to share their principles with others.

Major Maintaining areas

In a business, as well as personal life, there are many aspects of maintaining which are essential to success. Here are some of the major areas that need to be reviewed in any team during the course of a project, or teamwork assignment. Regard them as a checklist. How does your team rate out of 10 on each of the areas.

Technical maintenance

This is usually the first thing that comes to mind, where the work processes involve complicated machinery and technology. A good example is the way modern elevators are maintained. Most people have fears of being stuck in an elevator, and rightly so. However, the failure rate is very low, primarily because in hotels, office buildings, hospitals and shops there are regular maintenance checks.

Sometimes it takes a disaster to improve maintenance. Some years ago, in the US, there was a meeting of war veterans at a large hotel. Some of the members took ill and died. Investigations showed that the air conditioning was carrying a deadly bacteria, which became known as legionnaires' disease, after the veterans.

The result was that urgent checks were done on other air-conditioning systems, and it was realized that a major problem existed. Laws were passed to bring in planned maintenance of these systems. As a result, many lives have been saved.

Technical maintenance, therefore, is well regarded, and plays a vital role in all industries.

How well does your team score on this factor?

Product quality maintenance

The rise of Japanese organizations helped that country to become a major industrial power after the Second World War. This was primarily because of Japanese attention to product quality and maintenance. They adopted the statistical control ideas of Edward Deming, and applied them rigorously to reduce errors and improve quality. Within the space of 20 years, they changed the image of their products from 'unreliable' to establishing the world standard for reliability. This sparked a major effort in other countries to do likewise.

Many project teams have therefore been formed to improve quality. The results of this are now appearing not only in products but in services. It is good to see in hotels and public places that, for example, the toilets are quality-checked every hour. Likewise, we should expect and get quality assurances on food products, education services and hospital care. In hospitals, the quality system should work to ensure services that are delivered on time in all areas from cleaning to the operating theatre.

Now quality management and maintenance is being standardized under ISO systems, but systems are only as good as the people who operate them. How do you rate your team on its quality maintenance?

Safety maintenance

This area has become a major area for project teams and maintenance work. The cost of industrial and commercial accidents can be huge. This, combined with health and safety laws, have put the focus on improving safety. These are two external factors that have had an impact on reducing accidents. In most organizations, there are project teams in place on a regular basis, assessing how to keep the safety levels high. This is particularly so in high-risk industries such as petrochemicals and aviation.

How do you rate your team on this area of maintenance and what can be done to improve things?

Ethical maintenance

Over the last few years, more and more emphasis has been placed on the ethical responsibilities that executives and their companies have to the community. This includes everything from insider-trading issues to bribery and corruption activity. Ethical issues also include environmental ones, as well as policies on supporting the disadvantaged and the community in which they operate. Some entrepreneurs, like Bill Gates of Microsoft and others, have set up special foundations to distribute wealth based on what they feel are important issues, continuing the traditions set by individuals like Carnegie, Lever and Cadbury.

It is a vital part of any organization to have ethical guidelines and policy statements that people can support. Today, there are many project groups in operation to establish and maintain ethical practices. How is your company doing in this regard?

Customer maintenance

Maintenance is usually seen as a cost rather than a revenue-earner, although increasingly views are beginning to change. The value of maintaining customer loyalty is recognized as part of revenue generation. It costs far more to gain a new customer than keep an existing one. It is here that innovation, promotion and maintaining meet.

Retail stores increasingly have clear customer-relations policies that outline customers' rights, and this is part of maintaining good relationships. How does your organization score on maintaining customer goodwill?

Personal aspects

Maintaining your own skills and competencies is vital for any successful team member. However, team members can have different views on what is meant by Maintaining. On a management workshop, I got these responses:

John Anson, an information specialist with a publishing company, said,

> Maintaining, for me, is really about keeping myself up to date. It is easy to rely on the skills you have, and not look at what is happening elsewhere. I read as widely as I can, and attend at least one workshop a year to maintain my skills.

He felt that he spent a lot of time maintaining his company's administrative systems.

> Maintaining means ensuring the quality of what we do is at the highest level. This means we have to ensure our information is correct. I am now heavily involved in a project called 'data integrity', which maintains our customers' records.

Helen, who works in a health centre, said,

> I recognize Maintaining as a key activity. I see many patients who do not look after themselves as well as they should. I try to maintain myself by regular visits to the gym and eating a balanced diet.

The growth of gymnasiums indicates the time and money people are putting into physical fitness and personal maintenance. Likewise, the explosion in the number of health food and advice shops also highlights where the priorities lie. These self-development issues are increasingly driven by the 20- and 30-year-olds with discretionary money to spare.

When I talk to people about work issues, they all have valuable contributions to make on personal maintenance issues. Many of them said that maintaining their personal values and direction were the most important aspects, in a world full of diversion and opportunity.

Standards of Maintaining

There is no secret formula for success, but it is easy to lose what you have achieved. That is why Maintaining is such an important part of project management.

'We put a lot of emphasis on the Maintaining function,' said Phil Skerret, an engineer at a large manufacturing company.

> Obviously, we pay a lot of attention to keeping the machinery in good order, but we go beyond that. We look to maintaining high standards in all areas of our business. To us, Maintaining means ensuring we work in a safe environment, and providing a caring, healthy workplace, where terms and conditions are consistent with the values of the business.

Standards require that each member of the team, and particularly the team leader, focus on the standards, not just in one area but across all. To assist in this, the concept of benchmarking has become popular, to enable one organization to compare how it is doing with others. As mentioned earlier, for safety issues, everyone compares themselves with the Dupont standard, which for many years has been the measuring-rod.

Many organizations now publish their company charter on how they will conduct their business. This involves statements on how they will relate, not only to their staff but also to their suppliers and their customers. It sets out their policies on Maintaining. Marks & Spencer established such a charter many years ago. All staff members are trained in the company's policies, and they are required, as an integral part of their job, to uphold and maintain them.

Maintaining standards is crucial to any business, and both the medium and the message must be consistent. Often, we find in our work that what is promoted is not always maintained. For example, most of the world airlines promote safety as a key factor. Yet some airlines still allow smoking, despite considerable evidence that passive smoking is dangerous. They put money before the health and safety of their passengers. They fail to maintain a healthy environment.

This is clearly the case in most restaurants. Despite government words about healthy environments, it is very difficult to find restaurants in which you can have a meal without toxic tobacco smoke clogging your lungs. Both restaurants and the government are putting money before health.

Given that business is a function of who you trust, and who you believe, it is vital to develop the Maintaining area as a prime function. In so doing, you will be able to cross boundaries more easily, and become more trusted than others.

Key values

Maintaining is built upon a value system embodying what is regarded as important. All team projects should have meetings in which everyone present is asked to identify key values. We often find that teams are soon able to identify 10 or 15 areas of concern, ranging from health and safety issues to ethical and customer-relations issues. In the workshops that I conduct, I ask participants to think about these issues.

'We found the session we conducted on our core values most enlightening,' said, the senior manager at a travel company.

> We never thought about the subject in depth before. By doing so, we soon realized our business depends on Maintaining a wide variety of activities, including accurate customer records, our customer-care policy, our reputation for honesty and fairness and, of course, our own internal teamwork relationships.

They developed an action plan to reinforce and improve their Maintaining function, which included putting more effort into revitalizing old customer relationships. Their plan also ensured that all staff members knew the key governing principles of the organization.

Organizations with strong Maintaining characteristics

There are many organizations that focus on Maintaining value, principles and standards as a prime aim.

- Greenpeace is a classic example of an organization driven by the need to maintain world environmental standards. It is sponsored by people who have strong views on what should be upheld, and it recruits dedicated people with a high level of technical skill.

- Amnesty International is devoted to protecting political prisoners. It has strong principles, whereby the organization tries to maintain the rights of those being persecuted. Many other civil-rights groups carry out similar functions within their own national boundaries.

- Religious organizations are also very strong in the Maintaining role. As protectors of a faith, they stress the value of maintaining traditions and principles. Testament to this is that the Roman Catholic church is the longest surviving bureaucracy, outstripping monarchies by a long way.

- Some commercial organizations have strong Maintaining principles as well. For example, the Body Shop has made a feature of its principles and its commitment to supplying products that meet strict criteria. Also, the insurance and banking industries have put great emphasis on Maintaining the values of confidentiality and security for deposits made with them, although they fall short on many occasions.

- Museums and libraries are classic examples of organizations that maintain our heritage as a key aspect of their work. These institutions place emphasis on preserving knowledge, the culture and works of art.

- The UN and other similar organizations have a major role in maintaining world peace and assisting countries to work together.

- Remembrance organizations, such as the British Legion, the Veterans Association in the US and the Returned Servicemen's League in Australia provide a strong Maintaining role. Each year, each country identifies special days on which we can honour links with the past through 'remembrance days', for those who gave their lives in the defence of their country.

- The Salvation Army is an example of a voluntary organization that plays a major role in maintaining people's physical and spiritual well-being. Many who work in other social services organizations see their Maintaining function as a prime mission.

- The justice system, and the law and institutions and roles associated with it, are supposed to be built on the tradition of maintaining justice, but over the years many have come to question whether these bodies and people maintain what they are supposed to protect. Too often the victims of crime do not get justice because the judicial system puts precedence on maintaining the rights of defendants.

Ways of Maintaining in projects

Most work projects are established to introduce and develop new processes and products. However, the Maintaining function has a major role to play in all projects.

The process needs to cover a review of the support requirements of the team. That should make sure that there are no 'road blocks' in the procedures that have to be followed. To deliver products or services, a team will need 'maintenance' procedures to ensure that everything functions at an optimal level. Just as a car needs regular maintenance to ensure optimum performance, so does a team need its regular '5000-mile service'.

Money can be saved if the team works on its Maintaining activities. The first step is to organize a meeting in which your team can concentrate exclusively on the key issues. It is best to write to all team members in advance stating the objectives of the meeting. This will give everyone time to think through the key points.

A good starting-point is to ask the team members what the key areas are in which good teamwork needs to be maintained.

Put the list on a display board. This will serve as your agenda for the discussion. In a typical meeting, the issues raised will cover both the tangible issues relating to furniture and machinery, for instance, right through to Maintaining relationships within the team and with other teams.

Get the team to look at both the internal and the external aspects of Maintaining. This can be done by having team members draw the perceived links with both internal and external stakeholders.

EXERCISE

- Internal team links – ask the members to draw up a Linking diagram with people inside the organization, and to identify where the maintenance links needs strengthening.
- External to the team links – ask members to connect the internal diagram to the external one and make a plan on how to strengthen the external links.

How to work with Maintainers

Some people opt for work in the Maintaining area, others do not. This section offers guidelines on working with these people.

They will be quieter than many other team members, preferring to do a job in their own way without too many interruptions. They are usually conscientious people who can be relied on, providing they are given enough time.

Time is important in your relationships with such people. Do not expect instant answers. They like to think about issues in depth. So, before you meet them, let them know what you have on the agenda, and send them as much information as possible. They will read it and come prepared.

The other important factor to note is that people who are committed to a work preference that puts Maintaining top of the list usually have strong values and principles. This may be reflected in the kind of work that they choose. Such people often go into the caring professions, such as teaching, health work or representing colleagues via union activities.

Some will be more organized than others. They will be practical and creative in their approach. The key to working with them, on projects or elsewhere, is to understand what they value as important. This will often emerge in deeds rather than words, as they like to demonstrate their feelings by taking action. It may be a present or a helpful gesture, but it is indicative of their feelings.

Helping them by support in word and deed will be appreciated. In that way you will build up strong interpersonal links that will stand you in good stead when problems arise and you need assistance.

Summary

This chapter has outlined the vital role of the Maintaining function in any team or organization. It is central to a number of key factors, such as:

- safety
- quality
- trust
- confidence
- honesty
- security
- loyalty
- ethics
- delivery
- standards.

These are just a few of the words that can easily be taken for granted, but are essential for business success. The attention given to Maintaining determines how well the team and organization perform in these areas.

It is also important to look at the amount of time you give to maintaining not only technical matters, but relationship issues. The latter in the long run are vital to everyone's career.

EXERCISE

- How well are the Maintaining activities done in your organization?
- What do you need to do personally to improve your Maintaining work?

■ **CHAPTER ELEVEN** ■

Leadership Linking – focussing on the priorities

How effective are you?

Leadership by Linking is the key to modern management. I have worked with many teams and found that, in most cases, their problems are caused by links breaking down:

- between team members themselves
- between the team and its suppliers
- between the team and its customers
- between the team and other teams.

A team is only as strong as its weakest link. It is rare that teams fail purely for technical reasons. Usually, they fail because of poor links. For example, at a simple level, the communication chain breaks down when:

- someone does not pass on a message
- someone refuses to talk to another person because they disagree
- someone loses confidence in a colleague's poor work, and refuses to co-operate
- there is a communication breakdown, and people blame each other.

Linking is the responsibility of all team members, not just the appointed leader. In order for a team to succeed, all members must look at what each person can do better to link together. In particular, they need to look at how the team performs on each of the other eight Team Wheel work functions. Any team that links well can get the job done more quickly. In such teams you will invariably have high energy and excellent team spirit.

This chapter outlines the 11 main Linking skills, and shows how they can be used to improve personal performance and team effectiveness. Let us start with an example, of how one manager, with whom I was consulting, described the start of her day, and the way she tried to link her team members together.

FIGURE 11.1: The Margerison McCann Team Wheel

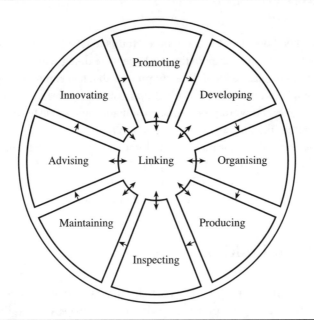

Leadership Linking in practice

I usually arrive at the office at about 8.00a.m. By 8.30a.m. the team arrive, and we start our half-hour meeting. During the meeting, we share what we are doing, and find ways to help one another. In this way there is a clear understanding of our priorities and pressures. My job is to encourage people to share key problems, and then to work out what we need to do to move things along.

These comments were made by Susan Menzis. When she took her first major management role she found that she was not particularly good at Linking. She did not have the morning meeting. Her basic preference was to concentrate on Organizing. She enjoyed setting the objectives, identifying who needed to do each task, and she made sure that a clear path was established. Once things were organized, she felt that everyone would do their job and the team would succeed.

Susan received feedback that people wanted to be more involved in the planning. After discussing this with some of her team members, she was also told that that there was a need for more teamwork, and less individualism. Fortunately, Susan recognized that she herself needed to do more team Linking, as she had previously dealt with members of the team on a one-to-one basis.

Susan said,

> That is when I decided it was important for us to take 15 to 30 minutes of the day to share and compare the work we were doing with one another. We were involved in a lot of different projects that had common elements. For example, we were often competing for the same resources, such as people's time, and word processors. So, it made good sense to share these points, rather than me always having to arbitrate.
>
> I have benefited enormously from these meetings. I have found I have more time to get on with the key projects, rather than having a trail of people knocking at my door. I also found that the team started to work in a more co-operative way, and their own Linking skills improved.

The eleven Linking skills

By observing the way people work in teams, we have been able to identify a number of key points that determine success and failure. As in the above example, there are a number of points, but in each situation we found one constant: the Linking skills of those involved. If practised by all team members, they enable the team to work as a coherent and effective unit. The Linking concepts are at the heart of successful team-work. Without them, the team usually operates well below its potential.

The 11 Linking skills are set out below. They are not set out in any order of importance. They are all important. They also represent two kinds of Linking:

- that which focusses initially on people relationships
- that which starts mainly with the task issues.

What effective leaders do – Linking skills

- Listen before deciding – active listening.
- Keep team members up to date on a regular basis – communication.
- Are available and responsive to people's problems – problem-solving and counselling.
- Develop balance in their team – team development.

- Allocate work to people based on their capabilities and preferences – work allocation.
- Encourage respect, understanding and trust among team members – team relationships.
- Delegate work when it is not essential to do it themselves – delegation.
- Set an example and agree high-quality work standards with the team – quality standards.
- Set achievable targets with the team but always press them for improved performance – objectives-setting.
- Co-ordinate and represent team members – interface management.
- Involve team members in the problem-solving of key issues – participative decision-making.

Susan Menzis realized that Linking skills were crucial to success in her job. By listening to her team, and facilitating the information flows, she helped them address the issues. She put more time into Linking her team together by focussing on all of the areas, but particularly the final one. She started to involve the members more on resolving key issues.

Types of Linking

The Linking skills listed above involve activities that require:

- the linking of people
- the linking of tasks.

The ones that put a prime emphasis on people-linking skills are:

- active listening
- communication
- problem-solving and counselling
- team relationships
- interface management
- participative decision-making.

The ones that put a prime emphasis on task-linking skills are:

- team development
- work allocation
- delegation
- quality standards
- objectives-setting.

Both types of Linking are essential for good team performance.

Internal and external Linking

Linking needs to be done both inside and outside the team. Effective management of both aspects of a team are essential if the team is to fulfil its potential. We refer to these as:

- internal Linking
- external Linking.

Managing relationships between the team and the external units, such as other teams within the organization and entities outside the organization, is called external Linking. If a team does not represent itself well to these external groups, it may well suffer from 'them and us' problems. This is when misunderstanding and conflict occur.

Internal Linking

In the course of our research, we have studied hundreds of teams. We have looked closely at the various strategies that they have employed for Linking their respective teams into effective units.

In all cases, where the team was successful, there was a clearly-thought-out approach that enabled people to co-operate and work together as a team. A significant part of everyone's time was spent on internal Linking. It involves the co-ordination of all team members, so that everyone knows exactly what is expected of them, and who in the team can help them at any moment.

CASE STUDY

Bob King, a sales manager for a company that supplies car accessories, found an interesting way to improve his team's Linking skills. He had a sales force of 140 people located in 20 different areas. He organized these areas into three major regions, and each of the regional managers had sales supervisors reporting to them.

The regional managers lived within their regions. Bob, whose office was located in the capital city, spent a considerable amount of time visiting the areas in each region. He believed that the only way to do his job properly was to see what the problems were in the field, and to talk with the sales representatives on a personal basis.

He said,

I believe I come to grips with the problems if I get out into the field and discuss the real issues. During the course of the year, I like to visit each area supervisor at least twice. It shows them that I consider their area to be important. On average, I make sure I spend a couple of days in each regional manager's office every other month, talking about their progress, sales, plans, budgets, staff development and other issues.

No-one can say I'm out of touch with what is happening. I know the sales territory as well as anyone. That is the way I keep everyone up to date. It's my way of making the sales team into an effective unit.

However, while Bob met with the managers, they rarely had a chance to meet and link with each other. They persuaded him to adopt a different pattern of Linking, whereby he held three area conferences each half-year with all the managers. These lasted a day and covered any issues people wished to raise. A major point raised at an early meeting related to Bob's external Linking. The supervisors wanted him to be more politically involved on their behalf in the organization, to get a larger budget. They also wanted him to be more externally focussed, and to meet major new clients.

The other benefit of this process was that it brought people in his team together to tackle problems, rather than Bob having to be the only Linker. However, by agreement, he still visited each area on a planned basis and the regional offices every other month.

Different levels

Many of the Linking skills are illustrated in this case, showing that to be effective a person has to operate at many levels simultaneously. Bob King felt that he put a lot of effort into internal Linking. He spent time visiting his team members and listening to their issues. He joined in the problem-solving and communicated his priorities. However, the team felt he needed to spend more time on external Linking, concentrating on interface management work.

In contrast, I was involved with another manager, working for a major US computer company, who had the opposite problem. He conducted a workshop with his managers, using the Team Wheel model as a focal point. He asked the members where they felt the team was strong, and also where it was weak. When it came to the weaknesses, they suggested his external Linking could be improved.

The manager asked for examples. Team members said that he spent too much time in the central office, and that he needed to meet key customers more often. Taking their advice, he agreed to develop a plan for more effective external Linking. As a result, he put more time and effort into meeting more clients with his managers. He put more effort into the active listening and the communication areas, plus participative decision-making and interface management. This was well appreciated both by his team and the clients.

Internal Linking charts

If the implications are negative, invite the team to draw up an action plan to improve the appropriate internal links. This can be a powerful exercise. When each person compares and shares their drawing and discusses the issues arising, it becomes immediately clear where they need to strengthen teamwork.

FIGURE 11.2: Team links

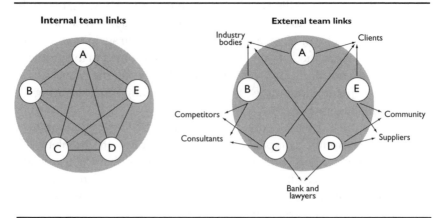

External Linking

No team can be successful by itself. The success of your team depends on Linking with other teams, and also key stakeholders, such as your clients. Some team members are likely to have a larger role in facing outwards. However, all team members should be ready to represent the team, and establish strong links with external contacts.

Look at your own job, and assess the external links you make on behalf of the team. These can include the following:

- being a member of an organizational committee
- representing the company at a conference
- being a member of a community organization
- meeting customers and clients
- negotiating with suppliers
- other roles in which you act as a representative for and on behalf of your team.

Management of these linkages is sometimes called 'boundary-riding', where various team members ensure that the best interests of the team are served when major decisions are made in these external entities.

When faced with a particular problem or opportunity, such as the implementation of a new project, it is important to take time and write down the external links necessary to make the project a success. To do this, it sometimes helps to conduct an analysis of external links.

Stakeholder links

The first thing to do is to list the key stakeholders in your team's work. It is surprising how often certain stakeholders are forgotten if such a listing does not take place.

A stakeholder is any person who has a 'stake' in the outcome of what the team is working on, in other words anyone who has a vested interest in the problem, opportunity or project, or who is in a position to influence the outcome, either positively or negatively.

It is useful to draw the lines between the internal person, or people, who make the links with the external contacts. You can indicate the strengths of the links between each person by drawing lines of different thickness, and, where the links are weak represent them with a dotted line.

Also, show any links that the external bodies have between themselves, and ask whether your team should be represented at those meetings. The important thing is to get all your team members to draw the external links and then compare notes.

It is the discussion that takes place on the drawings that is the vital element. In those discussions, the focus should be on the implications, in particular who will do what to strengthen or, if required, weaken the links. The success of the team will depend on the strength of these links. Take the drawings that are made seriously, and ask each person to explain their thoughts. It is a powerful exercise that can highlight many problems and opportunities.

External Linking in practice

One of the teams that I advised was in a large architectural practice. The senior partners reviewed their external links as part of a workshop on business development. For some time, they had been concerned at the relative decline in the number of contracts they were winning.

Their analysis of the team's external Linking shocked them. It showed that their senior people were more focussed on internal team matters. They had very few external contacts. Those they had were mainly with existing suppliers and builders. They had a few people on community projects and government committees, plus some charity and society meetings. They felt that that was insufficient for the commercial Promoting work that was required.

However, the problem had been staring them in the face for a long time. The previous year a senior partner had resigned unexpectedly, and took early retirement. He had been much criticized by many of his colleagues for rarely being in the office, and doing little architectural work. Indeed he spent most of his time wining and dining with clients or potential clients. He was out Promoting, but colleagues defined that as 'having a good time on company expenses'. Following his departure, commissions declined dramatically.

The board members now realized that they had relied too much on his external links to gain sales. They decided to allocate special responsibilities for external Linking amongst those present, and to invite people at other levels to contribute. As a result, the time allocation of people in the business began to change in the following ways:

- More time was spent on commercial relationships Linking.
- More time was spent on external Linking to represent the organization on public bodies and committees where connections could be made.

Gradually, the change in focus to Linking and Promoting began to pay off with an increase in contracts.

Balance in Linking

The important thing in any business is to respond to the needs of the situation. It is no use saying that there is one formula that will last forever. There is a regular need to review actual activities, and see what kind of Linking is necessary.

Some roles, usually by definition, have an orientation toward particular kinds of Linking. For example, sales and marketing roles would be expected to be more outward focussed. Yet, to succeed, those who work in such roles must build strong internal links to people in their organization who can deliver what they sell.

Likewise, people in operations, administration and production are more likely to be involved with internal Linking. However, to be effective they need to establish close links with those who are externally oriented and, where appropriate, be involved with external Linking.

Summary

This chapter has outlined the central importance of Linking in everyone's job. The 11 Linking skills provide guidelines for assessing and developing leadership Linking skills. In addition, look at:

- your current job and assess what are the Linking requirements
- your team, and assess the strengths and weaknesses of the links.

    Consider where you need to put more effort to be effective. Is it on:

- the internal organizational and team links?
- the external to the organization links?
- both internal and external links?

    Also, look at your career needs. In order to progress, where do you need to gain more experience? Should your next job involve more internal or external Linking? Indeed, what can you do in your current job to develop your internal and external Linking experience?

    Linking skills are the key to team-leadership success, and also to personal career success.

EXERCISE

- What is the balance between your personal internal and external Linking at present, and how should it develop in the next year?
- Share a diagram of your view of your team's internal and external links with colleagues, and discuss if any changes are required.

CHAPTER TWELVE

Team Linking – integrating and co-ordinating team efforts

Linking in practice

From the work I have done with various teams, it is clear that successful ones have a total view of teamwork: that is they pay attention to each of the major functions of teamwork outlined in the previous chapters. They do it professionally. Rather than reacting to a crisis, they establish a plan for dealing with the major teamwork functions, and then link them all together to make effective teamwork

Teams that are successful at Linking have a balanced performance around the Team Wheel. This chapter provides an in-depth example, based on a team that had considerable experience in project work. However, as you will see, the team experienced many problems because it did not have a common language, or teamwork system. You can use this as a case study to assess how you can apply the issues arising to your own teamwork.

The team was involved in R&D. It had problems in getting its ideas accepted by senior management, and its funding for research was in grave danger of being cut. In addition, there were also communication problems with those involved in the manufacturing part of the business.

In the initial discussion, which highlighted the need to improve communication, the team leader said, 'People don't really understand our work. Most of it is very complicated. You need to have a degree in science just to understand the language.'

The team had indeed received feedback from other departments that their clients had difficulties understanding their efforts. They were increasingly seen as being marginal to the business. My role was to assist in a review and plans for action.

The research team agreed to have a special workshop to discuss its role and contribution to the organization. This event was based on the key ideas in the TMS. We discussed how they could improve the team's work. Numerous ideas began to emerge. Throughout, the aim was to help team members become more effective at team Linking and co-operation, and to do this the Team Wheel was the focal point for understanding the issues.

This was done in two ways. The first was to look at the internal Linking within the team. The second was to look at its external stakeholder links, such as customers, clients, suppliers and other teams.

FIGURE 12.1: The Margerison McCann Team Wheel

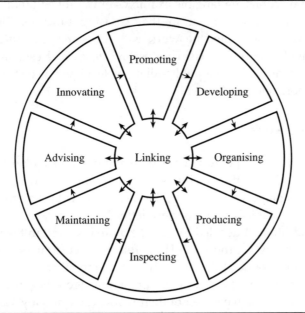

Advising work

The research team recognized that the information and advice that it provided to other groups within the organization was written in a language that was difficult to understand. Team members therefore agreed to present their proposals, and views, in a simpler language, relating specifically to the company's goals.

A project group was set up. Members of the marketing, sales, and public relations departments were invited. Later on, someone from the manufacturing area joined the group. The results were quite dramatic.

The project group examined how information was currently being disseminated, and then advised the team on how it should present its findings. It recommended short, one-page reports relating to the day-to-day business, rather than the longer, erudite scientific reports that were previously distributed. It also proposed changes to the annual research conference. This had been conducted in the same formal way for as long as people could remember. The project group recommended smaller meetings, in which people from different departments could discover what the research group was doing. It also recommended that the research group send representatives to meetings in other departments. In this way it could keep up to date with what was happening and maintain a regular flow of ideas between the various groups. As a result, the information exchange led to closer relationships and improved understanding.

These actions are tangible examples of improved Linking, but the result was an improvement in the Advising function. The people involved were the same, the work was the same, but attitudes and support made the difference. The research team had established links that worked, not only on a public-relations level, but also in making the research more relevant to users.

Promoting work

The research group openly recognized that it did a poor job of Promoting its research. Most of the brochures and representations were couched in technical language. As a result of the discussion with the project group, it decided to establish a regular newsletter.

In addition, it decided to become more involved in the marketing of the company's products. They felt that customers could then understand the value of the research being undertaken.

The result of this was that senior managers began to promote research as a distinctive aspect of their work. The company's advertising took a new approach under the banner 'the innovation leaders'. Suddenly, the research was at the forefront of the company's promotional image. The research division's function was no longer seen as a backwater of scientific study. It became central to the company's surge into the marketplace, with research as part of the leading edge.

Once again, the team had made the vital link between what it was doing and what others in the company, and particularly the clients, were doing.

Developing work

The research group had traditionally left Developing work to various marketing executives and project leaders. As a result of its re-assessment, it came to the conclusion that it had to follow through, and to be involved in, development work.

Members of the team were asked to take part in committees, to look at new product planning, and customer development and market research. Consequently, the research team gained a better understanding of the views of people who were dealing with customers.

On a number of experimental projects, they were able to involve at an early stage those in charge of product development and marketing. This resulted in the research being speeded up, because researchers could focus more on customers' needs. Again, the value of Linking with those who worked in other parts of the Team Wheel paid off.

Organizing work

For a long period of time, the research group had been regarded, by many people in the business as ineffective at organizing itself. Many jobs were never completed on time.

It was difficult to get researchers to take on supervisory work. This was seen by many of them as a promotion that gave them more money, but it took them away from what they enjoyed. They felt that they spent too much time on committees, writing reports and managing others. The researchers were also reluctant to take on non-supervisory administrative work at the expense of conducting research experiments. They saw this as a waste of time, causing them to miss out on their main career as scientists.

Meetings among the research people were conducted poorly. Few people attended. Also, poor organization reflected itself in cost over-runs in many areas. After discussion and assessment, the research group decided to look at how it could organize itself better.

Firstly, it conducted an action-learning assignment to identify the key areas of organizational procedures in need of improvement. This involved a study of what was required, through assessment of the action taking place. Also, many researchers attended time-management courses, and the whole group developed a focus on objectives-setting and benchmark evaluation. In addition, staff members were provided with training in interpersonal skills, how to run meetings, and aspects of teamwork. All in all, there was a sharper edge to the way resources and staff were organized.

Some members of the scientific team originally felt that this was going to be a waste of time, because it took them away from research work. But after three months they could see the benefit of a more structured way of operating. They took ownership of the re-organizing of their department, and within six months more projects were completed on time and within budget.

Producing work

Previously, the scientific team regarded their research as primarily an input activity. They concentrated on basic research. The message was: 'We cannot tell you when it will be finished, as research can't be subjected to a systematic production format'.

However, by involving people from the manufacturing section of the business in the planning of their research, two ideas were introduced. Systems, such as project planning and quality analysis – which had long been used in manufacturing – were introduced to the research department. They had an impact, and the research function became more effective at Producing work, achieving outputs on time.

Inspecting work

The work of the research group was strong on Innovating, but often seemed to be weak on Inspecting. It was felt that there was insufficient attention paid to details beyond the work required for experiments.

The scientific rigor was there, but there was insufficient emphasis on the practical implications. Very often, other groups in the organization would point out areas in which the practical utility of the research work was being overlooked. It was agreed that the Inspecting aspect of their work had to be improved.

Also, the research team had not worried too much about the financial aspects of its research work. Members always asked for more money than they needed, and when times were good they got the money. However, financial controls on spending were weak, and a lot of money was wasted. Following discussion with the internal accountants, they decided to introduce a system of auditing. This encouraged project teams to take responsibility for research productivity.

They introduced a number of leading indicators that related research results to costs. One interesting aspect of this approach was that the research group began to spend more time talking with internal colleagues, rather than seeing the external professional scientists as their prime audience. Once again, the value of internal Linking came to the fore in a practical way that had an impact on the way in which they worked, and results improved.

Maintaining work

The scientists regarded the Maintaining function as something that other people should do in the business. They never felt it was a prime area of their concern. Their job was to Innovate, which they saw as the opposite of Maintaining.

We initiated discussions on what Maintaining meant to them. The technical aspects they felt were important. Their research laboratories and facilities were rated as first priority, until the issue of safety was discussed. It was felt that more effort and attention was needed in this area, as well as with other aspects of the business. Maintaining quality and standards of research were also highly rated. However, they recognized the need to look at the way other teams dealt with these issues. A project group was established to look at these issues by comparing action with other groups. Once they started to make links with others, they began to improve in various aspects of Maintaining, and this had an impact on their output.

Linking

It is easy to assume that everyone in a team knows what is going on, but, in most cases this is not so. The internal links necessary for the team to work effectively are often missing.

The research group carried out an exercise in which it reviewed internal links, using an internal Linking chart. The results showed that several team members were not consulted when major decisions had to be taken. In addition, some team members had little knowledge of what the other scientists did, resulting in some duplication of effort.

Team members decided that it was important to have a voluntary one-hour Linking meeting once a week, chaired, in rotation, by each member of the team, including the more junior people. The topic for discussion was chosen by each team member, and circulated in advance. Although there was some concern that people would not attend, the idea was a great success. Six months after the initiation of the idea there was an 80 per cent attendance rate.

Summary

This example illustrates how team Linking can be achieved by looking at the Team Wheel. It indicates that in order for a team to succeed, it has to:

- examine all the teamwork function areas, rather than just one or two
- have the involvement of people from different sectors of the business to advise
- have team members cross borders, and to other teams to learn the way they work

- have the determination to transfer successful practices from elsewhere to their team
- have an emphasis on external Linking with other departments, whilst strengthening internal links
- look at the customer and client requirements as the starting-point for Linking and improvement.

The team in this example, with advice and guidance, improved its Linking and its performance. In the process, each team member learned a great deal about the other functions, Advising, Promoting, Developing, Organizing, Producing, Inspecting and Maintaining, and that assisted their Innovating work.

EXERCISE

- If you assess your own team on the teamwork functions described in this chapter, where is most effort needed in order to improve?
- What is the best way to get your team to focus on Linking activities?

■ **CHAPTER THIRTEEN** ■

Personal team work preferences – a road map for success

A practical tool for leaders and team members

This chapter looks at people's work preferences, based on Team Wheel functions. The work of the Institute of Team Management Studies gives access to over 130,000 contributors. This helps in an understanding of how work preferences compare. Knowing the major work preferences of your team will help you plan ahead.

Given the eight major teamwork functions described, do the majority of people at work prefer some of types of work than others? The answer is definitely yes. Therein lie some of the problems that team leaders have to manage. It is not easy to get a balanced team of people with work preferences that suit each task and every occasion. Even if it were possible, there is no guarantee that such a team would perform better than another, because skills and competence come into the equation, plus experience. But knowing the work-preference profile of your team's work can be a great asset to any manager.

The worldwide research on people's work preferences is described in chapter 16, and provides an excellent base for comparison and discussion. This information exists as a result of many hundreds of thousands of people completing our Margerison McCann Team Management Questionnaire. It is a 60-item questionnaire measuring work preferences on the Team Wheel. This assessment has been the cornerstone of our applications work.

For those people who complete the Team Management Questionnaire we are also able to provide each individual with an indication of how their work preferences compare to others in similar jobs, the same country, and of course age and gender differences. So far, in the region of one million people have been introduced to TMS, and most have received a personal profile.

This chapter indicates how it works in practice, and extends and supports the teamwork model. Work preferences are those interests and ways of working that appeal, and these are measured by the questionnaire. The results are presented in terms of the personal Team Management Wheel, which is shown below. This is an extension of the Team Wheel as described, as it refers to personal preferences rather than just work functions or tasks. Linking is measured separately using the Linking Skills Questionnaire, a multi-survey instrument, where other people assess your skill, so you can compare them with your own assessment.

FIGURE 13.1: The Personal Team Management Wheel

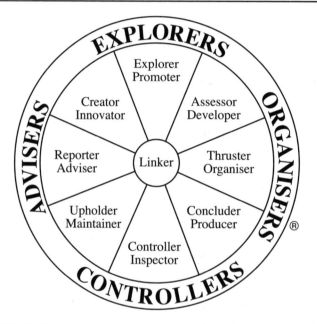

The actual terms used in the personal Team Management Wheel come from discussions with people in the workplace. For example, we discovered:

- People who enjoy Innovating work describe themselves as creative, so we derived the name Creator Innovator for those who enjoy coming up with ideas and experimenting.
- Likewise, those who enjoy Promoting often say that they see themselves as explorers looking for new opportunities, so we coined the term Explorer Promoter.
- Those who like Developing plans and processes say that they enjoy assessing ideas and opportunities. We call them Assessor Developers.

- Those who prefer Organizing people and resources say they like thrusting forward – to set dates, timetables and achieve results, so we refer to them as Thruster Organizers.
- Those who choose Producing as their main area of interest like working in a systematic way to conclude a job and to deliver, so we give them the name Concluder Producers.
- People who have a preference for Inspecting work say that they like to control details, and are able to audit procedures and processes. Therefore, the term Controller Inspector is appropriate.
- For those that choose to concentrate on Maintaining, the term Upholder Maintainer applies. Such people have strong beliefs and principles, and therefore put a premium on upholding standards and values.
- People who prefer to participate in an Advising role value collecting, sharing and reporting information, making the term Reporter Adviser relevant.

We found that not everyone wants to work in the same way. That may seem obvious, but until we had developed the Team Wheel, and the questionnaire, no-one could say for certain what the work preferences of a team were. Consequently, many teams were unbalanced. They had problems because they had some people who wanted to work on Innovating and Developing work, but lacked people who wanted to do Maintaining and Organizing work, or vice versa.

The reason for the differences is not just training and experience. It is because we have different interests. Some of that is based on personality factors, and some based on lessons of life. In the following section, we outline how you can understand the work preferences of your colleagues, and yourself.

How we measure work preferences

Work preferences are measured using four key scales that record major characteristics about people in the workplace. The original idea for these scales is derived from the pioneering work of Carl Jung on psychological types, described in his book of the same name (Jung, 1923). We have adapted the terminology to fit the modern work environment and measure the factors in that context. The main characteristics are:

Relationships preference choice

Extrovert   Introvert

Task approach choice

Practical   Creative

Decision mode choice

Analytical   Beliefs-based

Organization preference choice

Structured   Flexible

The four levels of work

While we can have interests in all of the above, people usually show an orientation to a particular end of each of the above scales. We can be extrovert at times, and introvert at other times. We usually prefer to spend more time doing one activity than another. The same is true for the other factors.

It is possible to ascertain your preferred team role by completing the Team Management Questionnaire (see appendix). It is the combination of all scores on the questionnaire that defines a preferred personal team management role.

For example, people who are extrovert and creative, and also analytical and flexible, usually enjoy Promoting. However, people with slightly different preferences also explore and promote. For example, those who prefer extroversion and creativity, and are beliefs-oriented and structured as well, usually enjoy Promoting work. Both are therefore known as Explorer Promoters.

Understanding others

It is useful to understand how you and others are likely to be influenced by your work preferences. Here is a summary of the roles. They can be helpful in your project work and teamwork activities.

Reporter Advisers

Reporter Advisers represent the classic advisory role on the Team Management Wheel. They are excellent at gathering information, and putting it together in such a way that it can be readily understood. If they are more introverted, they will probably rely on written formats for their information. If they are more extroverted, they will be good communicators, and probably rely on a network of colleagues and acquaintances for their data.

Reporter Advisers are people who prefer to make sure that they have all the information before they take action. This often causes others, particularly Thruster Organizers, to suggest they are unable to make up their mind, but Reporter Advisers will typically respond, 'How can I take action unless I have all the information?'

In contrast, those who prefer to be Thruster Organizers, may take action with only 20 per cent of the information, and sometimes find it hard to understand those who prefer the Reporter Adviser role.

Reporter Advisers do not enjoy conflict. They have 'antennae' that can detect a potential conflict well before it happens. Usually, they will move to defuse the conflict, or else position themselves well away from any direct effects. They can be invaluable in ensuring that there is thorough research on the information before implementation occurs. If a colleague with a Reporter Adviser role in the team says that they have something to say, then listen carefully. It may save a lot of time and money.

In the worldwide sample those with Reporter Adviser preferences constitute 3 per cent of team members.

Creator Innovators

Creator Innovators tend to be 'future-oriented'. They will enjoy thinking up new ideas and new ways of doing things. They are usually very independent, and they will pursue their ideas regardless of present problems, difficulties, systems and methods that might get in their way.

They need to be managed in such a way that their ideas can be developed without too many organizational constraints. Sometimes organizations set up R&D units, separated from production units, to allow these people to experiment with ideas. That can lead to poor links, but it can also be a way of getting dedicated attention on a new project. They may well say, 'How can I work unless I have all the ideas?'

Creator Innovators are sometimes accused (by their opposites on the Team Wheel) of 'having their heads in the clouds'. This is usually because they are looking to tomorrow, rather than worrying about today. They tend not to be structured in the way that they go about things, and may sometimes appear disorganized and absent-minded.

Some are more introverted, preferring to be 'back-room' people working on their own or in small groups, on important problems. Others are more outgoing, and can be zealous in their advocacy of ideas they really believe in.

In the worldwide sample, those with Creator Innovator preferences constitute 10 per cent of team members.

Explorer Promoters

Explorer Promoters are excellent at taking ideas and Promoting them to others, both inside and outside the organization. They enjoy being with people. They usually have an excellent network of colleagues to gather information and test out opportunities.

Usually they are advocates of change and are highly energized, active people with several different activities on the go at once. They enjoy being 'out and about'. They are good at finding contacts and resources, which can help the organization move forward.

Explorer Promoters are usually entrepreneurial in their approach, and persuasive. They are often influential, and can talk easily, even on subjects in which they are not experts. They are excellent at seeing 'the big picture', and for developing an enthusiasm for an innovation among other people. They may say, 'How can I contribute unless I look for new opportunities?'

However, they are not always interested in 'controlling' and 'Organizing' work. They may not pay sufficient attention to details. In this regard, they will often benefit from having a person who prefers to work as a Concluder Producer, or Controller Inspector, although they may sometimes have difficulties in interacting with these people.

Explorer Promoters enjoy 'off-the-cuff' conversations, and need to interact with others to be at their productive best. It is not for them to spend long periods in a 'back-room', working alone on their problems. They need people to provide the sparks of stimulation. In this regard, they can be energy-giving. Equally, though, their effect on others can sometimes be energy-draining, as meetings can last a long time.

Many Explorer Promoters have 'an eye for an opening'. They are quick to see an opportunity, and seize it before it disappears. Sooner or later in their careers they may get their fingers burnt, but this does not seem to worry them – they usually rebound, looking for the next opportunity. It is this characteristic, of course, that is essential for successful Exploring and Promoting.

In the worldwide sample, those with Explorer Promoter preferences constitute 10 per cent of team members.

Assessor Developers

Assessor Developers are located on the Team Management Wheel mid-way between the Explorers and Organizers, and they exhibit both of these characteristics. They may not always think up good ideas for themselves, but they are excellent at taking the ideas of others and making them work in practice. They are usually sociable, outgoing people who enjoy looking for new markets or opportunities. They take ideas and match them to opportunities, always mindful of the organizational 'bottom-line' constraints. They often make good product-development managers, and are also good at assessing new ventures. They may say, 'I need to look and assess and develop proposals before coming to a decision on how we should proceed'.

Assessor Developers usually display a strong analytical approach. They are at their best when analyzing and developing several different possibilities before decisions must be made. They like organizing new activities. They respond well to such challenges, taking an idea and pushing it forwards into a workable scheme. However, once the activity has been set up and shown to work, they will often lose interest. They will prefer to move on to the next project, rather than be deeply involved in the production and control of the output.

In the worldwide sample, those with Assessor Developer preferences constitute 17 per cent of team members.

Thruster Organizers

Thruster Organizers are people who enjoy making things happen. They are analytical decision-makers, always doing what is best to get the task done, even if their actions upset others. Their great ability is to fix and arrange things. For this reason, they are often found working in project-management-type positions.

They will 'thrust' forward towards a goal, meeting conflict head-on if necessary. They emphasize targets, deadlines and budgets, and will ensure that people are organized to take action. They may say, 'How do we need to get things organized in order to work effectively?'

Thruster Organizers usually prefer to work to a plan, and in a structured manner. They like objectives clearly set. In a leadership role, they will ensure everyone in the team knows what has to be achieved and when. They will set objectives, establish plans, work out who should do what, and then press for action. They tend to be task-oriented, but in their pursuit of goals may sometimes ignore people's feelings. This, more than anything else, gets them into difficulties with their colleagues, particularly those on the other side of the Team Wheel who want more time to consider things.

In the worldwide sample, those with Thruster Organizer preferences constitute 25 per cent of team members.

Concluder Producers

Concluder Producers are practical people who can be counted on to carry things through to the end. Their strength is in setting up plans and standard systems so that output can be achieved on a regular basis in a controlled and orderly fashion. For this reason, they do not like rapid change, as it interferes with the efficient systems that they have established. This may sometimes cause difficulties with their Creator Innovator and Explorer Promoter-oriented colleagues, who continually try to change ways of doing things.

For Concluder Producers, the challenge lies not in dreaming up new ideas but in doing work effectively and efficiently. They are often more patient than others with routine work, as their drive comes from a 'job well done'. As a result, they are sought after as managers, for their ability to deliver results by working in a quick, reliable and dependable manner. They may say, 'The job is not done until it is done in a systematic way that can be repeated'.

However, they may get into a systematic way of doing things, and resist change. Their motto is, 'If it isn't broken, don't fix it'. However, a person who is proactive will make links with others, irrespective of the immediate needs, and build up sound relationships to resolve problems as and when they occur.

In the worldwide sample, those with Concluder Producer preferences constitute 24 per cent of team members.

Controller Inspectors

Controller Inspectors are people who prefer to work more by themselves in a reflective way. They will probably focus on facts and figures and the detailed side of work. They are usually careful and meticulous. They can spend long periods of time on a particular task, working quietly and do not like to be disturbed. This stands in direct contrast to Explorer Promoters, who need a wide variety of tasks to engage their attention, as well as people with whom they can interact.

Controller Inspectors are comfortable working within agreed rules and regulations. They like to apply rules, and gain compliance, as they see that is the basis for order. They feel that people should follow the rules because they are made to ensure an organization works in the most efficient manner. For this reason, they often choose to work in situations where their output is guided by the organization or governmental regulations. Many people who prefer this approach work in finance, accounting and quality-control positions, where their 'Inspecting' preferences are important assets in the work they are doing. Others may gravitate to police work, or customs work, or security work. They may say, 'The important thing is to ensure that the details are correct, as half a job is not worth doing'.

The formulation and checking of contracts is an area that Controller Inspectors can do well, along with detailed computer systems, and issues on safety. As I have outlined in the chapter dealing with Inspecting work, there is a wide and ever-increasing amount of work in the control and inspection areas of business and government.

In the worldwide sample, those with Controller Inspector preferences constitute 8 per cent of team members.

Upholder Maintainers

Upholder Maintainers are people with strong personal values and principles. These are of prime importance in their decision-making. Usually, they have a high concern for people, and they will be strongly supportive of those who share the same ideals and values as they do.

They prefer to work in a control-oriented, supportive way, making sure that things are done according to their standards. In addition, they prefer an advisory role in the background, rather than a leading executive role. However, because of their strong principles, they may 'dig their heels in' when confronting issues that oppose their beliefs. They may say, 'The important thing is to have standards and to keep to them'.

They will not react in an extroverted, quick-tempered way, but in a quieter, more stubbornly resistant manner. This can sometimes be very irritating to Thruster Organizers. In fact, a meeting between a Thruster Organizer and an Upholder Maintainer may be like an irresistible force meeting the immovable object!

However, the Upholder Maintainer is an invaluable support member of any team, providing guidance and help on issues that need to be well thought through, especially in terms of principle.

In the worldwide sample, those with Upholder Maintainer preferences constitute 2 per cent of team members.

Linking

Linking involves all roles. Linking is not just a preference, but a set of special skills, as outlined earlier. The aim of an effective leader should be to link the team together in association with one or more of the work-preference team roles. The aim of team members is to link effectively with people in all areas of the Team Wheel that enable them to do their job well.

Summary

This chapter has outlined the personal implications of the Team Management Wheel as a tool that can be used in any aspect of project management. Personal preferences are very strong determinants of the way we work. To understand your own work preferences, and those of your colleagues, will enable you to have a better insight into how to link with others and how to communicate effectively with them.

EXERCISE

- In what areas of work, as described by the Personal Team Management Wheel do you prefer to put most of your effort?
- What are the areas in which you need to improve your contribution?

CHAPTER FOURTEEN

Do you need team balance? Assessing the team strengths

How to assess strengths and weaknesses

A winning team uses the talents and abilities of every player in a cohesive and co-ordinated way. Although one or two individuals may shine above the rest, in the end the team usually wins because it is well balanced, and all team members contribute and complement one another. But do you need a team with work preferences in all areas?

It is easy to see the concept of balanced teams in the context of sport. For example, consider a soccer team. It is no good having a team that is strong on defence but weak on attack. Equally, a sports team may fail if its players are effective on the left side but poor on the right.

So it is with work teams. You can apply the same sporting principles to the formation and operation of the projects and team. In each one, there is the exploring of opportunities, the creation of openings, and the effort to get the team members working in their best positions.

Some members will be better at controlling details than others, while some members can excel in finding new opportunities. In teams in which you have worked you will know that some people are better at Inspecting, while others are better at Innovating and others are strong on Organizing. Some may be effective in all areas. However, we have found that people prefer certain areas of work to others, and that is where they usually perform best.

Therefore, we have developed the concept of teamwork based on the front and rear wheels of a bicycle, as a way of showing the relationship between:

■ task work requirements
■ personal work preferences.

The Margerison McCann Teamwork Bicycle

FIGURE 14.1: The Margerison McCann Teamwork Bicycle

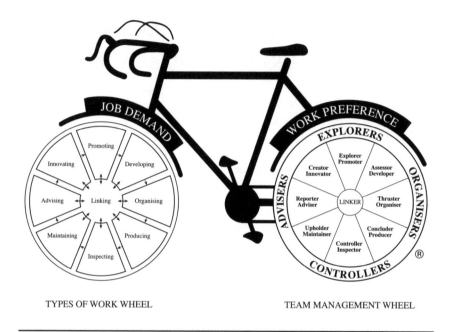

TYPES OF WORK WHEEL   TEAM MANAGEMENT WHEEL

This shows the task work functions on the front wheel, and the personal work preferences on the rear wheel. In that sense, the task work functions lead the way, giving direction, the personal work preferences provide the energy and support.

This is the vital question of balance between what the task demands and what the individuals in a team prefer to do.

The issue of balance is critical. For example, say you have a task that requires the main focus to be in the Organizing and Producing functions, yet the major personal work preferences of the team members are in the Innovating and Promoting areas. Clearly, there is likely to be an imbalance. What would you do in such circumstances?

It is a problem that regularly confronts teams and their managers. Task demands and personal interests and work preferences do not always coincide. Many managers know intuitively that there is an imbalance, but until they see the Team Bicycle model they are not likely to see the problem areas. Through this system, many managers have been able to diagnose what needs to be improved in their team. They gain both the language and team map to assess the action needed. Sometimes a remedy means recruiting new people, but most often it requires that existing people be given the training to widen their team contribution. Let us look at some examples.

Teams in banks

Many of the teams have greatly improved their performance by analyzing the balance in their team. Banks, for example, normally perceived as conservative organisations, have traditionally placed emphasis on the Inspecting, Maintaining and Organizing work functions. Their work procedures are designed to ensure that money is highly controlled and standards are vigorously upheld. As a result, the emphasis in banking for many years was towards Controlling rather than Exploring, with some exceptions in the merchant-banking fields, and the extension of credit-card access.

People who were selected and promoted within banking organizations often showed more of a preference towards the Concluder Producer, Controller Inspector and Upholder Maintainer parts of the Team Management Wheel. The aim of banks is to make a profit by providing confidence to customers, opening at set times, delivering a standard service according to a set of rules and procedures, balancing the books each day, and ensuring safety and security. This all favoured types of work in the south of the Team Wheel.

Those staff who preferred 'Explorer Organizer' tasks were given few opportunities to exercise their preferences. This changed somewhat when competition increased. Both existing and new banks were forced to challenge each other for business. Most managers and their teams were initially taken by surprise. There was a call for more effort on promotion and sales. The focus was widened for all managers, to encourage them to be innovative and development-orientated.

The response of banks to competition was a concerted effort to train their personnel. During one of the workshops, in which I was involved with a national bank, there was much criticism from branch managers. One of them voiced the feelings of many when he said, 'I did not come into this bank to be a salesman'.

He and other managers soon realized that they also needed to recruit people with different work preferences to complement the entrenched Controlling/Organizing culture that had been built up over many years. Many of the newly recruited people entering from other industries had both 'Explorer' and 'Organizer' preferences, encouraged by years of working in an environment in which survival depended upon identifying and developing the next opportunity.

Gradually the banks learned the need for different preferences in their teams, and they developed a new approach to teamwork. Now, a number of banks encourage people to get experience in all the sectors around the Team Wheel as they move through their careers. They are, therefore, given different jobs in various areas, as described by the eight major teamwork functions.

The production team

I worked in a factory team in which all the members' work preferences mapped into the Thruster Organizer, Concluder Producer and Controller Inspector roles. They agreed that they needed to improve in their Advising, Innovating and Promoting areas.

After discussion, they decided to focus some time on the Innovating sector of the Team Wheel. They hired me as a consultant to introduce some new perspectives into their view of the workplace, based on our TMS.

During the workshop, I encouraged everyone to consider any idea, however wild it might be. Each person was invited to put up an idea. It was quickly recognized that to pursue any idea there was a need to work in the Advising area to get relevant information.

Many project groups were set up to investigate and report on the feasibility of the ideas. One of the great learning points for me was the reaction of individuals. Some found it difficult to work outside their preferred area, where systems and procedures guided them. Others relished the opportunity to go out and ask questions, revelling in the ambiguity of not having a system, and not knowing the immediate answer.

The results were impressive. They developed new work practices and reduced costs. They increased productivity. In addition, project members found out more about their abilities using the Team Wheel as the framework. They proved that, whatever your work preferences, you can develop skills in many areas and contribute to all aspects of teamwork.

Marketing teams

I have worked with various sales and customer-service teams. These include teams in advertising and promotion, as well as sales and marketing.

As you may expect, the members of these teams often show a 'weighting' towards the 'Exploring' side of the Team Management Wheel. This is, of course, useful for the kind of work that they do. But a team that is totally made up of Explorers can have serious problems if it ignores the 'control' requirement. Whenever I have worked with these teams, I have encouraged them to examine their work preferences and discuss the implications.

In a sales team, the members discovered their work preferences were all in the Explorer Promoter, Assessor Developer and Thruster Organizer parts of the Team Management Wheel. Also, they agreed that they did not always 'link' in with the activities of other teams as much as they should. However, once they learned the concept of the Team Wheel, they realized that they needed to work closely with the:

- controlling part of the organization (provided by the administrative support team)
- Advising function (provided by the market researchers).

In this way, they achieved balance by externally Linking their team to two others on a regular basis.

If your own team is unbalanced, it can be important to look for creative ways to achieve balance. Often, the recognition of a 'gap' in the team is enough for the members to place extra effort into a particular area. But, this does not always happen naturally. So ask your team members to consider how they might 'stretch' themselves around the Wheel work functions to cover areas not currently high on their level of preferences. Also, discuss with the team whether external links to another group might bring in people with strengths in different parts of the Wheel.

Team balancing tips

Here are other ideas for consideration:

- select team members to complement those you already have
- make use of consultants on a part-time basis to plug any team gaps
- link your team to another team with skills in the areas you lack
- develop team members, so they are comfortable working in different areas of the Team Wheel
- structure team meetings, so that all parts of the Team Wheel are discussed and used.

For example, it can be useful to name and conduct the following,

- 'green' meetings to discuss information needs
- 'yellow' meetings to explore options
- 'red' meetings to decide action
- 'blue' meetings to check details and review progress.

Project team issues

If a project team is unbalanced, it will experience problems sooner or later. For example, a team of five or six people with 'Controller' preferences will tend to see the world in the same way. While they may be excellent at doing detailed and accurate work, they may not always see the wider picture, or develop ideas for the future. They may also be weaker on promoting opportunities, and in developing and implementing new products and services.

Similar imbalances can occur, of course, with other work preferences. Consider, for example, a team composed primarily of people with Explorer Promoter work preferences. A team like this is likely to enjoy discussing ideas and seeing how they can be used. They would also make numerous external contacts and be strong on influencing others. However, they may well miss details and deliver products or services that are incomplete and inaccurate.

On the other side of the range, a team composed of mainly 'Organizers' will, most likely, have problems because not enough time is spent gathering information on which to base decisions. They may rush into decisions before all the facts are known. Likewise, teams biased towards the Creator Innovator sector will usually come up with a lot of ideas, but not always have the skills and interest in seeing them through to a finished product. Teams that have mainly people with Reporter Adviser preferences spend a lot of time exploring options, but delay decisions until they are convinced that they have enough data. By then, the opportunity may have gone.

Balanced teams, however, encourage 'multiple descriptions and discussion' of the same event. These teams benefit from having a diversity of views to consider before making decisions.

Using the Team Wheels

The two Team Wheels can be used to assist any team. Sometimes, it helps to think of them as the wheels on a bicycle, as described above. The front, Types of Work Wheel helps define the key tasks and processes.

This can be a good checklist to help steer the team through all the tasks it has to accomplish, and to determine which ones need to be improved. The rear wheel of the bicycle, representing the personal work preferences of the team members, enables each member to discuss with the others how best to work together.

The power of teamwork comes through team members understanding each others' work preferences in relation to the tasks and the needs of others. Having people use their strengths in the right place is vital. For example, having Explorer Promoters involved in Promoting work, and Controller Inspectors involved in Inspecting work and so on, is an important principle of teamwork. But it is equally important that people are not limited to one area and constrained, or boxed, by having a name put on them. For career development and experience purposes it is helpful to work in areas other than those you prefer. The object of team management, and the Team Wheel approach, is to enable people to discuss with colleagues and contribute in the way that is best for them and the team.

Team Linking

A vital aspect of this is team Linking. It is only by linking members together, and enabling them to understand the different approaches, that the whole team will develop increased levels of respect, understanding and trust. Using the two Team Wheels in conjunction with one another, as described, will result in quality teamwork.

There are some interesting aspects to this.

- Task links: this is the Linking between the various activities that have to be done. It is a bit like handing on the baton in a relay race. Certain tasks have to be done before others. For example, on a building site the concrete base has to be laid before the carpenters build the infrastructure. However, certain tasks can be going on concurrently, such as the marketing of the construction. As in any project, there should be a plan and a schedule of activities. Linking them in order and sequence is a key job. Never underestimate the value of planning and sequencing, vital aspects of Linking.
- Internal and external task links: this involves both internal links with colleagues and external links with suppliers and clients. It is often at the boundary that the problems occur, where you do not have authority or control in someone else's system. That is where personal external links become vital if the contractual task links are not working as they should.

Success requires both task links and interpersonal links to work together.

Task and personal work preference Linking

This is the extent to which people's preferences match up with the tasks that have to be done. At certain stages of the task Creator Innovators may need to be in the driving seat. This, for example, is the case when designing a new building, and the ideas and imagination can flow. At the next stage, people with strong Controller Inspector and Assessor Developer preferences are needed on the job, as you negotiate contracts and buy the materials. Then you will need the people with Thruster Organizer and Concluder Producer preferences involved in the construction work.

None of this is to say that people with other preferences cannot do these kinds of work. However, if the preferences line up with the task requirements, it is likely that there will be a better fit. Energy and interest will line up with the task.

Throughout there is the need for Linking. At the task level, it is the plan that provides the links, but when the plan and the contracts do not work, high-level team problem-solving and Linking skills are needed to keep a job on track.

The two Team Wheels provide a framework to assess on both the task level and the interpersonal level where effort is needed. In such situations, ask yourself what the Linking problem is. Is it that the plan is not working because there is a flaw, or is it that the people are not able to work effectively on the tasks due to a team imbalance? It provides a good way of diagnosing the situation, and the basis for working out what to do.

Summary

This chapter has outlined the two Team Wheels:

- one with the task focus
- the other with the personal work preference focus.

If the task involves all the Team Wheel functions, it is vital to have a balanced team, both in terms of work functions skills and competencies and personal work preferences. Where this is not so, it may be possible to have a team that has preferences in just a few areas. It is the understanding of how both Team Wheels can work to the advantage of the organization and the team members that can create a powerful impact. The two wheels provide a strategic map for:

- planning
- the recruitment of people
- the allocation of resources
- the use of time
- the management of people.

The common denominator to both wheels is the Linking function. Success depends on how the team task aspects and the personal work preference aspects link together effectively. Taken together, they are a powerful set of tools for managing not only teams and projects, but also your own work activities to achieve first-class performance.

EXERCISE

- How well balanced is your team in terms of the way it performs its tasks?
- What needs to be done in your organization to get the task aspect and the personal work preference aspect of teamwork, as illustrated in the two Team Wheels, to work together well?

CHAPTER FIFTEEN

The language of teams – enabling the team to work together

Sharing the same language

To improve teamwork, you need a shared language. Only in that way can people communicate and build up ways of trusting each other and solving problems. The Team Wheel provides a language and system of communication.

The eight key work functions plus Linking explain the key activities that have to take place in any team if it is to be successful. In our work with various teams, this has become clear, and the examples described here outline the way in which the language is used in work teams.

Let us start with an example. Jane Barnes is a product development manager for a large multinational food manufacturer, which has been using TMS for a number of years. Her view is that

> TMS is a language that helps us all work as a team. Most of us are members of multi-functional teams. We only come together for certain projects and then disband. Sometimes we are a team for only a few months, and most often we belong to two, if not three different teams at the same time. The TMS approach helps us move forward more effectively. The first thing we all do is to share our preferred roles on the Team Wheel. Understanding each other's work preferences encourages respect for all, and helps us to diffuse any conflict that may arise.

Coloured meetings

Another example is that of a new team in the petrochemicals industry. It met and shared members' team profiles at its first meeting. Members all

THE LANGUAGE OF TEAMS   143

had major work roles in the Organizing and Producing sectors. They also had work preferences that aligned with this type of work. They recognized this as a strength, but they also discussed their weaknesses, and noted that they did not always have the necessary information to hand when making decisions.

They decided to institute a number of Adviser, or 'green', meetings. The rule for a green meeting is that discussion has to focus on the information required for the current projects:

- What is required?
- Who will get the data?
- How will reports and plans be made?
- Who should be involved?

The green meeting was followed with a yellow, or Explorer-type, meeting, in which the team explored all the options that could possibly be considered for the current project, rather than racing off and implementing the first solution that came into their mind.

Here the focus was on:

- What options do we have?
- How can they be tested?
- Who should be consulted?
- What promotion do we need?

Having an understanding of the different approaches, and how they differed from their own strengths enabled members to gain a better review of information and options before moving into Organizing and Controlling modes, their areas of strength.

Team differences

To make progress, take time to assess and understand the differences between team members. For example, in a construction engineering team regular conflict occurred. At a meeting, the Team Wheel was discussed, and each member completed a Team Management Questionnaire, from which could be produced their own personal team profile.

The team had a range of work preferences, with one Creator Innovator, one Explorer Promoter, one Thruster Organizer, one Concluder Producer and one Controller Inspector. However, they had great difficulty working with one another, mainly because they all had different ways of approaching work.

The marketing manager, whose main preference was an Explorer Promoter said,

> I have found it difficult to relate with our accountant. I feel he is over-critical. He wants to consider everything in detail before making a commitment. However, now that I know that he has a preference to work as a Controller Inspector, I can understand why he behaves the way he does.
>
> TMS has given me a language with which I can communicate with him. As an Explorer Promoter, I often get carried away with ideas, but now I know I have to research my ideas more before presenting them to him. I usually write things down and send them to him for consideration. I've also learned to contain my energy and enthusiasm when interacting with him, and to slow down the rate at which I speak, as he likes to consider the details and take one point at a time.

Linking guidelines

The language of teamwork is especially important when Linking and co-ordinating your work with others. I have found that team members find the concept of Linking very valuable in improving their communication.

While it is valuable to understand one's own work preferences, it is even more useful to understand the way in which to link with others. This section summarizes the guidelines that have been produced for accredited members of TMS. These are people who are trained to use TMS in workshops, where they are trainers and facilitators. The guidelines are valuable to all team leaders. These notes provide a useful checklist for developing your influencing skills, and improving your team communications.

- How to link with Explorer Promoters

Expect them to:	Ways to respond
Explore ideas	Ask questions in order to understand
Look for opportunities	Ask for examples
Concentrate on the future	Ensure that they link with other areas
Be enthusiastic	Look at the practicalities
Be optimistic	Test realities and get things in writing
Open to new approaches	Follow up leads

- How to link with Assessor Developers

Expect them to:	Ways to respond
Focus on a plan	Understand their plan
Want to test ideas	Provide a practical test
Budget	Provide figures
Move things forward	Suggest a system

- How to link with Thruster Organizers

Expect them to:	Ways to respond
Be organized	Set out your objectives
Be factual	Be in command of the facts
Be punctual	Be on time
Be action-orientated	Have action proposals, not just problems
Be impatient at times	Indicate your concern if being rushed

- How to link with Concluder Producers

Expect them to:	Ways to respond
Be output-focussed	Find out their deadlines and work to them
Be practical	Be ready with the facts
Work to a plan	Understand it before changing anything
Be time-conscious	Be on time and use time well

- How to link with Controller Inspectors

Expect them to:	Ways to respond
Concentrate on details	Provide relevant data
Require an agenda	Indicate the topics in advance
Be on time	Keep to the point and time deadlines
Work to a system	Ask them to indicate the requirements
Focus on how to control things	Ensure that they are controlling the right things
Want time to work alone	Do not interrupt unless it is urgent

- How to link with Upholder Maintainers

Expect them to:	Ways to respond
Consider matters carefully	Provide full information

Have strong values	Find out what their values are
Uphold standards	Ask them for their criteria
Be practical	Look at existing operations

- How to link with Reporter Advisers

Expect them to:	Ways to respond
Ask questions	Discover their interests
Value research	Take an interest in their work
Take their time to do a good job	Set deadlines well in advance
Have views that might be different	Listen and consider

- How to link with Creator Innovators

Expect them to:	Ways to respond
Have lots of ideas	Invite them to discuss ideas
Want to experiment	Provide cost and time deadlines
Be independent	Give freedom for expression
Be flexible	Help with systems and structures
Try new approaches	Assist them with tests and trials
Challenge the status quo	Ask for evidence and performance

The above short summary outline complements the main points in this book. It brings together the ways in which you can take your own work preferences and establish better links with colleagues and clients.

Note that no-one is locked into any of the team roles. Most prefer one or two. In order to work with colleagues and clients effectively, you need to know their main preferences. If it is appropriate, ask them to complete the Team Management Questionnaire. Then you can not only understand their approach but also work with it. This is the key to modern teamwork. It involves mutual understanding. Beyond that, it involves mutual support and assistance. Once you know your own work preferences, you can begin to work with others, so that they see you as Linking well with them. Then both your contributions will improve.

Linking and the language of teamwork therefore go together. One assists the other. To link effectively, you need to know the language of others in terms of their work preferences, but equally to have a clear understanding of the language of their tasks. For example, it is vital that if the task demands Maintaining and Inspecting activity the language and approach relates to that, rather than, say, Innovating and Promoting. By understanding the dynamics of teamwork, you can then adjust your language and behaviour to the needs of the business situation.

CASE STUDY: TEAM LINKS AND CO-OPERATION

Barry Smith, of HR Strategies, one of the accredited members of TMS, specializes in the start-up, renewal and turnaround of executive teams using TMS. Working with the top team of an international news organization, he found that the manager criticized the team's inability to take the initiative. The members were likewise critical of his meddling in their areas of responsibility when following through the creative initiatives that he had started.

Barry introduced them to the Team Wheel in order to provide a framework for discussing the issues. Each team member was given a Personal Team Management Profile. The manager's preferences were mainly a combination of Creator Innovator, Reporter Adviser and Explorer Promoter. He realized as a result that he needed to work closely with those who had complementary work preferences. For example, a hitherto underutilized team member – a person with a great preference for working in an introverted way, with high Concluder Producer and Controller Inspector preferences – was found to be the most effective linker between the leader's charisma and the team's need for clear action plans.

Barry noted that over a period of time, once the manager and his team understood the implications of their own teamwork preferences, and those of their colleagues, they learned to work together more effectively. The team was invited to join him in the early stage of generating options. As a result, they understood them more clearly, and became more effective in the operational strategies and outcomes. For the manager, this meant delegating more after the creative stage, letting his team get on with delivery.

CASE STUDY: THE POLICY REVIEW TEAM

Another example outlines how one group perceives its work in the context of the Team Wheel, and the need for strong links between all members. The staff in a Department of Transport and Communications of a national government, responsible for reviewing policy in a number of areas, met in study groups for about six months to prepare a working paper on government initiatives for the next few years. The group then disbanded, and the members re-formed into other teams, with different membership, for each particular policy area, so teamwork and the understanding of a system and work preferences were crucial.

We were asked to help improve their teamwork. A key part of this was introducing the team management language of the eight major work functions and Linking. The following is a summary by a member of the use of the TMS approach.

> The TMS language has allowed us to get up and running very quickly. We recognized the major components of teamwork in the Team Wheel. We discussed them at our first meeting, where we examine our policy project through the eyes of the Team Wheel.
>
> Firstly, we discussed what information and advice we needed, and with whom we were going to consult. Next, we looked for new ideas associated with the technology concerned. We talked with many researchers about future trends, and then we assigned Innovating tasks to various people. We also promoted our ideas to key stakeholders in government and industry. We became better external linkers. In this way, we gained feedback on the general level of acceptance, which led us to developing a practical framework.
>
> We set up deadlines, to make sure that the work was completed on time. Policy matters are sensitive to political debate, and therefore it was essential that we focussed on the Inspecting work function. Usually, one of our team, with preferences closest to that of Controller Inspector, was assigned the task of checking all the details and calculations. A major mistake could cost a politician their job.
>
> We also made sure that we addressed all the Maintaining issues of the project by ensuring the spirit of the paper reflected the current societal thinking around important values, such as environment and energy. In addition, we tried to ensure that everyone was linked together throughout the whole project, by holding weekly meetings, which everyone was expected to attend.

Team members' responsibility

Today, it is expected that team members take responsibility for their own way of working and learning. The key to success in business is to ensure that teams work effectively and efficiently. As indicated, that requires a common language, and focussing on the two Team Wheels can drive your team forward. A starting-point is to examine the nine key team performance factors and assess how your team is currently performing in relation to them. These have become for many teams the guiding factors, as well as the common shorthand language for diagnosing problems, suggesting solutions and getting action.

It is easy for members, once they know the system, to use the nine factors of:

- Advising
- Innovating
- Promoting
- Developing
- Organizing
- Producing
- Inspecting
- Maintaining
- Linking.

It is a great help when the problems of Producing and Promoting are being discussed and all team members immediately can picture the Team Wheel. They can then start thinking of how to get the internal and external Linking to work effectively.

Also, mapping team members according to their preferences on the personal Team Management Wheel highlights the strengths of the team. It helps you manage team processes better, and gives you an understanding of why conflict arises.

If you want to improve your Linking skills, you may choose to have these assessed by your colleagues, and compare them with your own views. This can be done by using the Linking Skills Questionnaire. This helps you develop an action plan for improvement, so that you can quickly become a first-class Linker based on the views of those with whom you are working. In so doing, the language of teamwork helps the process of problem-solving.

Summary

This chapter has outlined how the Team Wheel, and the associated functions, are now an integral part of the language of many organizations. That helps to speed communication and understanding between team members. The results show in the quality of their outputs and productivity. As so much work today depends on good service, the Team Wheel and the profiles can make a real difference to performance. They are the means by which people link together more effectively, and this shows in customer service.

The TMS approach has proved a reliable and useful basis for developing business operations, teamwork and personal development across industries, countries and cultures. It combines a problem-solving system with personal understanding of team work preferences.

EXERCISE

- With whom do you need to share the ideas in this book in order to gain action and improvement in leadership and teamwork?
- What is your personal plan for development in the nine key areas of Team Management?

CHAPTER SIXTEEN

Research findings – the research facts and figures

How people see their work preferences

The research on which this book is based involves over 130,000 people. This chapter summarizes the main statistical findings on the eight major work functions and Linking skills. This has been used on a worldwide basis, as the systems outlined have been applied in over 150 countries and translated into 15 languages.

Key team performance factors

A summary of the teamwork behaviour factors are listed below, with a short definition for each. In addition, the eight work functions are integrated, using the important concept of Linking.

- Advising: gathering and reporting information
- Innovating: creating and experimenting with ideas
- Promoting: exploring and presenting opportunities
- Developing: assessing and planning applications
- Organizing: organizing staff and resources
- Producing: concluding and delivering outputs
- Inspecting: controlling and auditing contracts and procedures
- Maintaining: upholding and safeguarding standards and values
- Linking: co-ordinating and integrating the work of others.

This system of teamwork has been tested rigorously on a comprehensive worldwide programme, involving over a million people. The TMS has been used in diverse cultures, including:

- North and South America
- Europe
- Arabia

- Southeast Asia
- Australasia
- China.

Areas of application

In particular, it has been used in economically developed countries such as France, Germany, Singapore, Australia, the UK and US, and in countries with substantially different cultures, such as Malaysia, Saudi Arabia, Papua New Guinea and Fiji. Teams in all types of industries have been researched, to find out what makes the difference between high- and low-performing teams. The nine key factors that emerged are the basis of outstanding teamwork. These activities are those used every day at work, but previously they have not been put into a team language system. The system has been used by commercial organizations, government agencies, voluntary organizations and community groups. It has been used by various professional mountaineering teams climbing Everest, and other peaks, to help improve their teamwork.

The Margerison McCann Team Wheel

The worldwide data

The principles of the Team Wheel and the associated feedback instruments have been available for over 10 years. So far, over a million people have used the system in their work, and over three-quarters of million people have gained personal feedback via the team profile.

This is practical book with the emphasis on team project management, but it is worthwhile concluding with a look at the main findings emerging from worldwide research. The following is a brief summary of the full data available from the Institute of Team Management Studies.

The questionnaire

The whole system's basis is called the Team Management Questionnaire (in certain countries called the team management index). It enables each person to indicate on a psychometrically validated measure their preferred way of working over the eight major work functions described in this book. As a result, each person receives a personal 4000-word Team Management Profile, which provides information on their work preferences.

This questionnaire has been used on management and team development activities, and over 129,000 people have contributed to the research results. This is therefore one of the largest and most comprehensive surveys of work preferences ever undertaken. It provides a rich insight into what people from different countries, professions and industries want and expect from their work.

Key contributors
- Total participants   129,818
- Industries represented   75
- Professions represented   227

Regional areas and participant numbers
- North America   33,984
- Europe   11,120
- UK   17,219
- Africa   1794
- Latin America   1994
- Southeast Asia   1770
- Northeast Asia   1222
- Australasia   52,064
- Middle East   293

Some of the functional areas
- Managing director/CEO   1365
- Personnel/HR/training   8259
- Sales/marketing/PR   11,932
- Finance/accounting   6753
- Production/construction/control   11,936
- Consultancy   5383
- Administration   12,461

Findings

The findings have major implications, not only for individuals and their careers but for the way organizations go about their business, for example the way they recruit, select and train. If an organization has a bias towards selecting people who are strong on Innovating, but do not like Organizing, Producing and Inspecting, then the business will need to look closely at how it keeps a balance of operations.

Equally, if an organization recruits mainly people who favour Producing, Inspecting and Maintaining, what are the implications for their future? In the early stages of an organization, you would expect there to be a large proportion of Innovators. Likewise, when a company is well established you would expect there to be a high proportion of Producers, generating regular outputs. Getting the balance right, therefore, is important. In this context, it is interesting to look at the worldwide figures.

Major role preference distribution for the worldwide sample (129,818 participants)

FIGURE 16.1: Role preferences

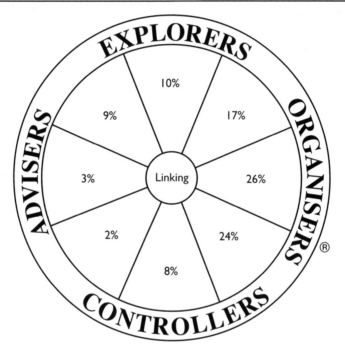

The areas referred to in the model are:

- Advising preference   3%
- Innovating preference   9%
- Promoting preference   10%
- Developing preference   17%
- Organizing preference   26%
- Producing preference   24%
- Inspecting preference   8%
- Maintaining preference   2%

It is clear from these figures that organizations tend to recruit people who are more orientated toward Organizing, Producing and Developing. In all, these account for two-thirds of the total.

It is interesting to note that those who have a preference for Promoting make up 10 per cent, and those who prefer Innovating, 9 per cent. This stands in contrast to those who favour Inspecting, 8 per cent, and those who favour Maintaining, only 2 per cent, and Advising, 3 per cent.

Country differences

The success or failure of business operations has been attributed by some to cultural differences, particularly in work values. It is interesting to look at cultural differences from the standpoint of work preferences, albeit that the figures are drawn not just from those of ethnic origin in the region, but some expatriates and immigrants. The figures below are percentages based on the eight key work functions.

	NA	UK	Eur.	Africa	LA	ME	Aus.	SEA	NEA	W
Advising	3%	3%	3%	1%	1%	1%	3%	2%	1%	3%
Innovating	11%	9%	10%	4%	5%	5%	9%	6%	4%	9%
Promoting	12%	10%	13%	6%	6%	6%	10%	6%	7%	10%
Developing	18%	17%	23%	23%	21%	20%	15%	19%	18%	17%
Organizing	24%	27%	25%	36%	37%	32%	26%	29%	34%	26%
Producing	21%	25%	19%	26%	24%	28%	26%	30%	30%	24%
Inspecting	8%	8%	5%	3%	5%	6%	9%	6%	4%	8%
Maintaining	2%	2%	2%	1%	1%	1%	2%	1%	2%	2%

- North America, including Canada (NA), is the second-largest group, with a sample of 33,984, and it has a relatively balanced distribution compared to other regions.
- United Kingdom (UK), with 17,219 participants, has a very similar pattern to North America, with a slightly higher emphasis on Organizing and Producing, which may support those who favour the stereotype of British bureaucracy.
- Europe (Eur.), with 11,120 people represented, has a similar pattern to the UK, with a slightly higher emphasis on the Promoting and Developing functions, and a slightly lower emphasis on Producing and Inspecting.
- The figures for Africa have a large proportion from South Africa, and the outstanding figure is the 36 per cent of people whose main preference is Organizing. This is well over one third of the 1794 people involved. Also, note the relatively low preference for Innovating. If this is replicated on a wider scale, it could suggest some organizational and new product problems have to be confronted.

- Latin America (LA), with 1994 people represented, has a somewhat similar profile to Africa, with a high emphasis on Organizing and relatively little interest in Innovating and Promoting compared to some other regions.
- The Middle East (ME), with 293, is a small sample, but indicates some interesting trends with 80 per cent of the preferences in three areas of the Wheel.
- Australasia (Aus.), with 52,064 people, is the largest group and has a similar pattern to the UK sample.
- Southeast Asia (SEA), with 1770 respondents, has a heavy emphasis on Developing, Organizing and Producing, which account for 78 per cent of work preferences.
- Northeast Asia (NEA), with 1222 people, has a heavy emphasis on Developing, Organizing and Producing, which account for 82 per cent of work preferences.
- Worldwide (W) percentages obviously reflect the larger number of participants from North America and Australasia, but it is interesting to see how the other regions differ considerably from the worldwide average scores.

Industries

People are attracted to certain industries because of the opportunities, not just for a job. That is, where they are more likely to find work that meets their work preferences. The data from the people in the following industries indicate where they see the main work demands in their jobs.

Worldwide Industry	n	1	2	3
Public Service	1613	Advising	Promoting	Organizing
Consultants	722	Innovating	Advising	Promoting
Banking/finance	686	Organizing	Promoting	Maintaining
Education	329	Advising	Maintaining	Organizing
Retail	305	Maintaining	Organizing	Promoting
Oil/petroleum	194	Advising	Maintaining	Promoting
Telecommunications	187	Organizing	Advising	Maintaining
Professional bodies	175	Producing	Inspecting	Maintaining
Manufacturing: general	164	Organizing	Maintaining	Advising

The rank order for the highest scoring between the above industries in each of the eight areas was:

- Advising: oil/petroleum
- Innovating: consultants

- Promoting: banking/finance
- Developing: consultants
- Organizing: banking/finance
- Producing: professional bodies
- Inspecting: professional bodies
- Maintaining: retail

Whilst an overview does not give the full picture, it provides an insight into how people in our sample see the major demands of their jobs. The overall pattern shows considerable variation. However, the role of Advising is regarded as critical in many jobs, as is Organizing, Promoting and Maintaining.

CEOs

A lot of attention is given in books and articles to the work behaviour and characteristics of chief executives. Of the 1365 worldwide CEOs who contributed to the work preference research, it is noticeable that they significantly differ from the total worldwide sample in their preferences for Developing work. Notably, 25 per cent of them rated this as a major role preference, compared to only 17 per cent for the worldwide figures, as shown below.

CEOs' self-perceived work preferences and job demands

	CEO Preferences	People Worldwide	Differences (1)	CEO Job Demands	Differences (2)
Advising	3%	3%	0	12%	−9
Innovating	12%	9%	+3	15%	−3
Promoting	15%	10%	+5	19%	−4
Developing	25%	17%	+8	11%	+14
Organizing	26%	26%	0	18%	+8
Producing	15%	24%	−9	6%	+9
Inspecting	4%	8%	−4	5%	−1
Maintaining	2%	2%	0	13%	−11

Given that the Developing function concentrates on planning new business applications and transferring ideas into an action framework, it is understandable that this is a high-scoring area. The highest-scoring area is Organizing, which is equal to the worldwide average.

The scores in the 'differences (1)' column reflect the percentage differences between CEOs' scores and the worldwide sample of over 129,000. The major areas of difference in addition to Developing are in the Producing and Inspecting areas, where the CEOs have a noticeably lower work preference score, and Promoting, where CEOs have a higher work preference score.

The 'job demands' scores are those that emerge from a sample of 100 CEOs responding to another validated questionnaire based on the same eight major work functions. This questionnaire asked them to identify the critical factors in their job. As this is their perceived view of what their job demands, we have called this the 'realistic' score, in contrast to what might be called the 'idealistic' score based on their preferences.

This illustrates some very interesting gaps, as highlighted in the 'differences (2)' column. It seems that the CEOs feel that they have to give far more time to Advising, Innovating, Promoting and Maintaining than they would like. In terms of their preferences, they want to concentrate for the main part on Developing, Organizing, and Producing.

Above all, any CEO needs to be strong on Linking and relating effectively with people in all the work functions to make the organization succeed.

Men and women

Much debate has raged in the press and journals about the different ways men and women are supposed to work. Our worldwide sample suggests only modest differences in their work preferences, as the percentages show below.

	Men	Women
Reporter Advisers	2%	4%
Creator Innovators	10%	9%
Explorer Promoters	11%	10%
Assessor Developers	18%	16%
Thruster Organizers	26%	26%
Concluder Producers	24%	25%
Controller Inspectors	8%	8%
Upholder Maintainers	2%	2%

For both 70,971 men and 44,368 women, the main preferences, accounting for 68 per cent and 67 per cent respectively, are in the Developing, Organizing and Producing aspects of work.

Dominant preferences

We measured people's work preferences on a number of important criteria. These are shown below on bipolar scales.

Work relationships preference

Extrovert   Introvert

Task focus preference

Practical   Creative

Basis for decisions preference

Analytical   Beliefs

Approach to Organizing preference

Structured   Flexible

In reality, we choose all of these factors to some degree in our work. However, most people prefer to choose more of one factor than another. The Team Management Questionnaire provides a measure for work preference choices. The percentages shown on the Team Wheel are derived from research on this questionnaire.

For example, one person may look for work in which they can exercise their extroverted, creative, analytical and flexible preferences. Another person may choose jobs where they can exercise their introverted, practical, analytical and structured preferences.

The worldwide findings suggest that on balance the percentages for people who prefer to work in the following ways are:

- more extroverted than introverted
- more practical than creative
- more analytical than beliefs-based
- more structured than flexible.

The extroverted, practical, analytical and structured emphasis is consistent with a strong Organizing preference. Also, because there is a relative balance between the extroverted and introverted scores, the second-highest-scoring area is Producing, consistent with an introverted, practical, analytical and structured preference.

Professional differences

We all have a stereotype of various professions. For example, accountants are often called 'cautious', and sales representatives usually seen as 'optimists'. Such characterizations reflect not only our perceptions, but to a certain extent their work preferences. For example, salespeople often prefer to be more extroverted and flexible, and accountants more introverted and structured in the way they work.

Some of the findings from the research in this respect are most interesting, as the following summary shows. Overall, the comparison shows that in a hierarchy of work preferences the rank order from the selected following professions are:

- Engineers   2256
- Accountants   1184
- IT and managers   586
- Teachers   525
- Project/production engineers   354
- Programme analysts   316
- Solicitor/lawyers   280
- Project managers   204
- Nurses   178
- Research scientists   121
- Chemists   104
- Librarians   104
- Scientists   103

Rank highest scores

- Extrovert preference: project managers
- Introvert preference: librarians
- Practical preferences: nurses
- Creative preferences: scientists
- Analytical preferences: research scientists
- Beliefs-based: none, but teachers came closest
- Structured preferences: project managers
- Flexible preferences: none, but librarians came closest

Age

It is often said that younger people do not have the same attitudes to work as older people. Are younger people different from older people when it comes to work preferences?

The findings show that the older people are the more likely it is that they will prefer a slightly more introverted form of working, with younger people preferring to be more extroverted. Also, there is an indication that the older people get the more likely they are to prefer a practical, rather than a creative, approach to work.

It is also noticeable that older people tend to be more driven by beliefs in their work, and prefer being slightly more structured than younger people. Overall, perhaps the preference towards a more introverted, practical, beliefs-based and structured approach to work characteristic of older people reflects a certain conservatism that comes with age.

Linking skills

Beyond individual work preferences there are Linking skills. Although a person may prefer to work in the Innovating area, for example, they will have to link with others to ensure that they understand what is required of them, and to be able to gain support for the application of their work. We developed a special instrument called the Linking Skills Questionnaire to measure people's Linking skills. This can be completed not only by the individual but by colleagues. In that way the person can receive a Linking Skills Profile that enables them to get the perceptions of others, which can be very helpful in discussions on ways to improve. Over 17,000 people have contributed to the research worldwide.

Do others judge a person's Linking skills higher or lower than the individual themselves? The figures below provide some challenging and surprising answers on the 11 areas selected. There are 5799 self-ratings and 11,346 ratings by others.

Mean satisfaction percentages

	Self	Others
Active listening	79.89	84.20[1]
Communication	81.46[2]	83.48
Problem-solving	81.74[2]	83.86
Team development	79.16[3]	82.20[4]
Work allocation	80.14[5]	83.22[6]
Team relationships	80.48[3]	82.19[7]
Delegation	80.35[8]	83.52[9]
Quality standards	83.60[2]	85.68[10]
Objective-setting	77.01[11]	80.91[12]
Interface management	79.68[13]	82.61[14]
Decision-making	82.77[15]	83.47[16]

Notes

1 n=11,345	5 n=5792	9 n=11,330	13 n=5787
2 n=5798	6 n=11,315	10 n=11,340	14 n=11,326
3 n=5796	7 n=11,336	11 n=5783	15 n=5785
4 n=11,327	8 n=5793	12 n=11,295	16 n=11,312

It is interesting to note that the individuals, on average, rate their Linking skills high, with all items over the 75 per cent mark. However, what is surprising is that the colleagues of the individual rated them higher on the particular skills than they did themselves. This would suggest that feedback from others can be the basis for useful discussion and confidence-building.

Team assessment

A similar comparison was also conducted to see how teams assess themselves, and how supervisors assess them. For this, we created the Team Performance Questionnaire, a specially constructed and validated instrument using the eight major work functions referred to above on work preferences.

Satisfaction averages were extrapolated and indicate how those involved felt the team to be performing in particular areas. The relationship is marked with a '−' symbol if the score is less than that which the team itself gave, or a '+' symbol if it is more. Where there is less than a 0.5 per cent difference, a '=' symbol indicates no real difference. There were 439 teams involved, with 120 co-worker and 306 supervisors ratings for comparison.

Mean satisfaction percentages

	Team	Co-worker group A	Supervisors
Advising	76.11	81.10 +	77.21 +
Innovating	74.15	76.03 +	72.97 −
Promoting	74.19	75.19 +	72.93 −
Developing	76.51	77.99 +	77.32 +
Organizing	77.65	75.68 −	77.64 =
Producing	82.22	81.17 −	81.40 −
Inspecting	79.17	79.47 =	79.65 =
Maintaining	81.19	81.96 +	83.99 +
Team Linking	75.93	75.99 =	78.25 +

This suggests that this approach to team assessment and development can pay dividends, if managed in a positive way.

Implications

The research findings indicate that the following are important for people at work. There are benefits to:

- understanding and using the nine work functions in the TMS, essential for the total running of a business
- gaining an understanding of one's own work preferences, and seeing that they relate to current work and future plans
- sharing and comparing one's way of working with colleagues within the context of the model, through the work preference profile
- gaining experience widely on each function of the Wheel in order to contribute effectively, wherever required
- developing, through experience and training, excellent Linking skills, so as to work closely within the team, with colleagues, and externally with clients and suppliers
- comparing perceptions of individual and team performance with significant others, such as supervisors and co-workers, as a basis for improvement.

Summary

In order to perform effectively, a team will need to cover each of the work functions. Most of the individuals and the teams worldwide, studied show people with work preferences that are stronger on the key functions of Developing, Organizing and Producing.

The eight major work functions provide a solid base upon which to assess a team and an organization. It has also proved a significant system for assisting in management and organization development work. At one level, it provides a strategic framework for planning, doing and reviewing performance. At another level, it is a guide to individuals on the issues to be considered in their career and day-to-day work.

Appendix – Team Management Systems instruments

Team Management Systems is a range of products and services covering the whole spectrum of expertise in teamwork and team management. They are designed by leading international management consultants Dr Charles Margerison and Dr Dick McCann.

TMS can be used in several ways to suit the requirements of the individual and the organization, as shown in figure A.1 that looks at the personal, the job and the team aspects.

The measurement instruments relating to the above issues and areas are:

- The Team Management Questionnaire (TMQ): this provides a valuable self-assessment of work preferences. It can be used by an entire team to build an overall picture of the strengths and areas of team preference, and improve team performance, or it can be used by individuals to provide feedback on their own strengths and weaknesses, and give direction for personal development.

  Responses to the questionnaire are analyzed by computer, after which you receive a 4000-word Team Management Profile containing information about work preferences, leadership strengths, interpersonal skills, decision-making and team-building skills.

- The Type of Work Questionnaire (TWQ): this is a 64-item questionnaire that analyzes a job in terms of the eight types of work functions. The report shows those elements of the job that are 'critical' to job performance. A match can also be made with Team Management Questionnaire results, to show the percentage overlap between a person's job and work preferences.

- The Linking Skills Questionnaire (LSQ): this is a 66-item questionnaire, measuring an individual's 'Linking' ability in terms of the 11 Linking skills. It is a multi-survey instrument that analyzes data from the

FIGURE A.1: Team Management Systems resources

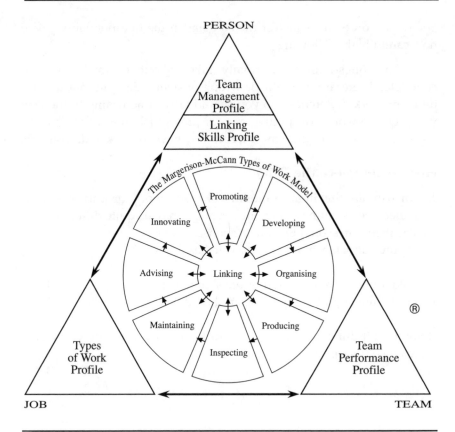

person whose Linking skills are being measured, as well as from various colleague groups, including supervisors and team members.

The output is a profile that graphs 'satisfaction rates' for each Linking skill and produces a narrative report recommending areas for improvement. The instrument allows a 360-degree view of all those people who interact with the person being surveyed.

■ The Team Performance Questionnaire (TPQ): this is an instrument that analyzes team performance and indicates how satisfied a team is with the nine team performance factors. It is a multi-survey instrument that gives a team feedback on how it is perceived by other teams, customers and clients.

The output shows satisfaction rates for each factor and also gives advice on specific areas of teamwork that might need improvement. The instrument also allows a 360-degree view of all those people who interact with the person being surveyed.

The Team Management Questionnaire

Before you proceed to answer the 60 items in the questionnaire, please note carefully the following.

This questionnaire normally takes about 10–15 minutes to complete. There are no right or wrong answers. Each individual has different work preferences, so you should answer according to the way you prefer to work, irrespective of your present job, the way you think you ought to work, or the way you currently have to work to do your job.

How to complete the TMQ

1) Answer all the items in terms of your work or career – your preferences at home or in your social life may be quite different.
2) The items are scored by your responses.

Your decision should be indicated as follows:

	A	B
If you definitely prefer A, your score should be:	2	0
If you definitely prefer B, your score should be:	0	2

If you find it difficult to decide which statement you prefer, you would score one of these:

A	B
2	1
1	2

2–0 (or 0–2) or 2–1 (or 1–2) are the only possible combinations of each item. Only whole numbers may be used. Do not allocate half numbers. You must make a choice one way or the other, no matter how marginal your decision may be. All items must be answered.

Example item:

	A	B	
I like verbal presentations			I like written reports

Example responses:

	A	B	
	0	2	I much prefer written reports
	1	2	I prefer written reports but like verbal presentations
	2	1	I prefer verbal presentations but like written reports

| 2 | 0 |

I much prefer verbal presentations

Please answer all 60 items this way.

Remember to answer ALL items 2–0 (or 0–2) or 2–1 (or 1–2)

A   B

1. I like to be convinced by the facts

I like to be convinced by people's view of what is right and wrong

2. I like to explore many different options, even if it means delaying action

I like to make sure that action is taken quickly to resolve problems

3. I like to emphasize the facts in explaining a decision, as people respond best to logic and reason

I emphasize beliefs in explaining decisions, as people work harder for things they believe in

4. I prefer to work with as much information as possible, and will not always be orderly

I prefer to work in an orderly way so I know where things are

5. I prefer working on complex problems

I prefer working on straightforward problems

6. I find talking things over with others helps me come to decisions

I prefer to be left alone to come to decisions

7. I actively search out theories

I am a practical person and do not spend much time theorizing

8. I probably take longer than others to make decisions, because I like to gather as much information as possible

I am probably quicker to make decisions than others as I like to see action and results

9. On balance, I am more outgoing

On balance, I am more quiet

10. Logical analysis comes first with me

People's feelings come first with me

11. I often change my mind at the last minute

I attach a high value to planning ahead, and dislike changing my mind at the last minute

12. When making decisions I often rely on 'gut feeling' rather than spending much time analyzing the situation | | When making decisions I usually analyze the situation fully rather than rely on 'gut feeling'

13. I prefer more of an organizing role to an advisory role | | I prefer more of an advisory role to an organizing role

14. I find it requires a special effort to mix with people I do not know well | | I find it relatively easy to mix with people I do not know well

15. I prefer possibilities | | I prefer realities

16. I like work which involves a high degree of visibility such as making presentations at meetings | | I like work which involves low public visibility, where I can do my work in my own way

17. People may describe me as 'down-to-earth' because I prefer the common-sense approach | | People may describe me as having 'my head in the clouds' because I am often dreaming up new ideas and new ways of changing things

18. I try to keep my personal feelings to the minimum when work decisions have to be made | | My personal feelings and beliefs are important influences in my work decisions

19. When organizing my work, I usually come to temporary decisions and revise | | When organizing my work, I usually come to a decision and stick to it as far as possible

20. In a group at work, on average I would talk less than others | | In a group at work, on average I would talk more than others

21. I plan work to avoid the unexpected wherever possible | | I often leave things unplanned and respond well to the unexpected

22. I often come up with new ideas but I don't always know how to make them work | | I usually know how to make things work but don't always come up with new ideas

23. I am easy to get to know, as I like meeting lots of people | | I am fairly quiet and people don't always know the real me

24. I prefer clear rules so that everyone knows what to do and work is completed correctly □□ I prefer fewer rules and procedures, so that changes are easier to make when needed

25. I come up with my best ideas working in a group □□ I come up with my best ideas when working by myself

26. I emphasize getting ideas □□ I emphasize getting facts

27. I usually let my heart rule my head □□ I usually let my head rule my heart

28. Attention to detail is the most important part of the work process □□ Attention to creativity is the most important part of the work process

29. I think I am basically a person of reason □□ I feel basically I tend to rely on my own opinions and views

30. I prefer to work in depth on a few issues at a time □□ I prefer to work widely with many issues at a time

31. I ask 'Is it fair?' □□ I ask 'Will it work?'

32. I rarely allow deadlines to be altered □□ I often allow deadlines to be altered

33. I prefer to work on tasks in which I can use my existing skills □□ I prefer to work on opportunities in which I have to develop new skills

34. When under pressure, I prefer to have time for myself to think things through □□ When under pressure, I prefer to meet with others to talk things through

35. I prefer to take things as they come □□ I prefer to work to a clear schedule

36. Solutions become clearer to me when I relate them to my beliefs □□ Solutions become clearer to me when I relate them to the facts

37. I usually see the whole problem but often miss the details □□ I usually do well with the details of a problem but often find it difficult to see the complete picture

38. I speak a lot, and this helps me think □□ I think a lot before I speak

39. Under pressure, reason must come before personal principles □□ Under pressure, personal principles must come before reason

40. I like to experiment with ☐☐ I like to solve problems in a
    new ways of doing things   practical, systematic way

In items 41–60, which word in each pair best describes you

41.	Persuade	☐☐	Consider
42.	Future	☐☐	Present
43.	Question	☐☐	Faith
44.	Imagination	☐☐	Common sense
45.	Orderly	☐☐	Flexible
46.	Production	☐☐	Research
47.	Belief	☐☐	Reason
48.	Concentration	☐☐	Variety
49.	Facts	☐☐	Principles
50.	Talkative	☐☐	Quiet
51.	Unplanned	☐☐	Planned
52.	Feelings	☐☐	Analysis
53.	Creative	☐☐	Practical
54.	Implement	☐☐	Support
55.	Control	☐☐	Explore
56.	Understand	☐☐	Decide
57.	Objective	☐☐	Subjective
58.	Build	☐☐	Design
59.	Careful	☐☐	Impulsive
60.	Action	☐☐	Information

A Team Management Profile example

Name: James Day
Organization: Day Corporation
Major role: Upholder Maintainer
Related roles: Thruster Organizer, Explorer Promoter
Key preference areas: Exploring, Organizing, Controlling, Advising
Your personal team management profile provides you with information about your work preferences. It is a starting point for consideration and discussion of how you approach your work and your interactions with others in the workplace.

Your own work preferences have been derived from your responses to the team management index. While you may work in any of the areas of the Wheel, your highest preference area, or major role, has been identified, together with two related roles which indicate your next-highest preference areas. All the roles are displayed on the Team Management Wheel. The 'Linker' role at the centre is the responsibility of all team members.

Your preferred approaches to work are measured on the four different scales: how you relate to others; how you gather and use information, how you make decisions; how you organize yourself and others.

How you relate with others

How you gather and use information

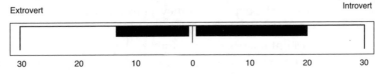

How you make decisions

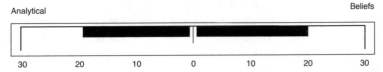

How you organize yourself and others

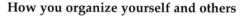

Structured   Flexible

30   20   10   0   10   20   30

Your responses to the Team Management Questionnaire are shown on the preceding bar graphs. For example, on the first graph the shaded area to the left indicates the extent to which you relate to others at work in an extroverted way. The shaded area to the right indicates the extent to which you relate to others at work in an introverted way.

By subtracting the lower score from the higher one for each area, you can see that, in your own case, your major preferences are more inclined to be introverted, creative, beliefs-based and structured.

Note that the Team Management Questionnaire measures work preferences, not skills – you may have good abilities in areas of work where you have low preferences.

Overview

Upholder Maintainers play an important role in any work team. Their main concern is to set up and maintain standards. They establish close and supportive relationships with those who uphold the beliefs and values they consider important. However, they can at the same time be tough opponents of people who they perceive stand for ideas and decisions to which they are opposed.

Upholder Maintainers can, therefore, be key people in generating ideas and views on how an organization and individuals should do things. The term Upholder Maintainer is consequently very appropriate for this important team role.

Work preferences

As an Upholder Maintainer, you will have quite a number of creative ideas which you will interpret through your own values. Where your theories combine with your beliefs, you have the powerful ingredients for taking and Advising on action. As you prefer an organized and structured way of doing things, you will usually move to put your plans into practice rather than just thinking about them.

Where your work and beliefs are closely related, you will work extra hard and have confidence in what you are doing. Contributing extra hours in such a situation is part of the challenge. Where your ideas do not support your beliefs, you may not be as highly motivated.

Often other people do not realize how hard you are working because you prefer to do a lot of your best work by yourself. Indeed, you have the capacity to concentrate for long periods of time and to persevere when problems appear. However, you like to balance these intensive periods with lighter moments when you can meet and interact informally with your colleagues.

You may well enjoy working on community activities, where you can contribute to the welfare and well-being of others. This could be through helping children, the elderly, a sports group or some other public cause.

While you will not enjoy being pushed, you can and do work to deadlines. Above all, you take a pride in the quality of your work and will ensure that it is done, not only to time but also to a high standard.

You will probably have a strong feeling of what is right and wrong, and will align yourself closely with people of similar beliefs and convictions. Your ability to 'read' people's motives and intentions is something that is important. You can often 'see' their strengths and weaknesses, and emotional makeup soon after you have met them.

You will have a vision of how things should be and will work towards it in a purposeful way. You can work for long periods by yourself in planning and preparation. Overall, you respect other people's feelings and work for what you believe is right, despite opposition on economic or other grounds.

Leadership strengths

As a leader, the Upholder Maintainer will deal with matters in some depth. Your strength here will be in your ability to grasp a wide understanding of the complex issues at stake, and to commit tremendous energy and effort to push for new approaches.

You try to establish an harmonious, close-knit team, and will spend time with those with personal problems or emotional upsets if you believe that they can benefit from your support. While you can be helpful, you can also be tough when required.

As a leader, you will set goals based on your ideals and theories, and will quietly but persistently pursue your objectives. You try to form a group of people who will support and work with you, but if all else fails, you will press on alone. This is particularly so when you really believe in the purpose of the activity. You may, therefore, take leadership in various social and community groups whose ideals and values you support.

Not everyone, however, will appreciate your leadership style, because much of your best work is done by yourself. Indeed, you often enjoy experimenting with new ideas, and may not share these until they are well advanced or fully formed. Your colleagues may then have difficulty in understanding how you came to reach your conclusions.

Your enthusiasm is a key strength. You don't believe in letting today's disappointments get in the way of tomorrow. Your ability to come up with new ideas and your optimism will usually engender confidence. However, you will probably react badly to personal criticism and dwell on it rather than accepting it and pressing on.

As a team leader, you can represent and defend the group when you believe that the issues are worth fighting for. At this point, you can become a negotiator and representative who is hard to beat. You will particularly support those who suffer from what you regard as unfair and unjust treatment.

You will normally adopt a quiet approach to leadership, but will let people know where you stand. You like jobs to be finished on time, so that everything is left neat and tidy. You will press for a high work standard and will not let people get away with slipshod work. Indeed, some will at times say you can be very critical when people do not meet your high standards.

You exercise leadership by doing rather than just talking and expect others to follow your example. You will probably talk in depth only with those whom you trust. At times, others may say you don't confide in them.

To what extent do you have special, group, problem-solving discussions on the key questions facing you at work? Such discussions give everyone on the team the opportunity to understand your concerns and express their views. Experienced managers have learnt that this is a useful way of getting people's opinions, even though specific criticisms may emerge. If handled constructively, such sessions can lead to major improvements. However, they need to be held separately from normal business meetings.

Decision-making

Your approach to decision-making is heavily influenced by your beliefs and values. This, combined with your imaginative ideas and concern to get things done in an ordered way, will mean that you push for action.

On occasions, however, you may take decisions too quickly. You will rely too much on the inspiration of the idea, together with the strength of your beliefs, and will not acquire sufficient information to assess the decision.

In the main, you will have a steady approach, together with a highly intuitive, creative way of gathering information. You are likely to see the world from a very personal, unique viewpoint. Your approach will enable you to reflect quietly and deeply upon matters. This, combined with your creative insight, will often allow you to see possibilities and ideas beyond the facts of the situation.

Other people will not always see the world in the same way as you do. Indeed, they may talk a lot but not really come to grips with the points you feel are important. Your own preferred way of working is usually to listen to what others have to say, but not make a major contribution yourself until you have clarified in your own mind the key points. In general, you like to understand the 'whole picture' before committing yourself. You are usually better able than others to see how things relate and interact, although the specific details and facts may be of little interest to you.

Taking into account your own concern to resolve and conclude matters, rather than generate a lot of extra data, this can sometimes lead to you being impatient with others who either don't share your vision or will not commit themselves. While you prefer to work in a co-operative way, your keenness to implement your ideas can sometimes be seen by others as being 'over-enthusiastic'.

You can indeed be extremely keen in your own quiet way, and will work for long hours to pursue the job in hand. You do not like to be beaten and will put in tremendous effort if you believe the issue or task is worth doing. You will not easily be thrown off course, and can be seen by others as stubborn and obstinate when it comes to changing direction. Essentially, you tend to have commitment to your ideas and the overall purpose, and do not like to be put off. Clearly this is a strength, but it needs to be played in the context of other people's willingness to go along the path that you have decided.

Interpersonal skills

Establishing sound interpersonal relationships is important to you, and you usually take time to do this well. You can be particularly concerned for other people's feelings and worries, and like to please and help those in need.

In your own way, you take time to work closely with people and try to understand their concerns. Wherever possible, you will seek to help colleagues and friends, particularly when they are having difficulty in career and work issues. You can often see the potential in others that they may not see or appreciate in themselves.

When you get to know people, you can find the right words to give feedback and encouragement. Your enthusiasm for what you are doing usually rubs off onto others in the team. In return, you will value those who appreciate your efforts, and make it clear by word and deed. Working in a supportive team will be important to you. Where it does not exist, you will seek to create it, or if that is not possible you will probably move on.

You can, therefore, work well with those who recognize your concern to support and help. You probably indicate more than others your appreciation of work well done. However, you can be critical when people do not pull their weight or pursue a course which is not the one you believe is correct.

Overall, you can provide a sound basis for improving interpersonal relationships not only in your team but between groups. You have a concern to uphold and maintain relationships, and will work hard to bring people together. Occasionally, those you support may let you down. They may play on your good nature, and you will have to make hard decisions as to whether you continue to help and support them and cause risk to yourself and the company.

You can be an effective representative of the organization when asked to 'stand up' for those things in which you believe, providing you have had time to prepare. On such matters, you can be an effective spokesperson or negotiator. Where, however, you do not identify with the purpose or cause, you will find it difficult to perform such roles with conviction. Play-acting in that sense does not come easily to you, when it cuts across your beliefs and convictions.

Overall, you can generate a high degree of enthusiasm and optimism among your colleagues. You also consider it important for established customs to be upheld and for recognition to be given for service and loyalty.

You can usually communicate well, particularly in the written word, where you often find the right phrase to capture the moment. This can provide the basis for you to involve others in your ideas and ideals, and get them as enthused as yourself on what can be achieved with collective efforts. You can also communicate well orally, particularly when you have had a chance to prepare.

Team-building

You prefer to have a close group of colleagues who share the same values as you. Establishing a solid *esprit de corps* is important. You feel people will want to give of their best if they have an harmonious understanding and help each other. You will, therefore, listen to what others have to say and will at times 'bend over backwards' to accommodate their points of view, to hold the team together.

To achieve a balanced team, it is important to have people working with you who have the required skills, but may not share your vision or ideals. To complement your own strengths, you may need to select Controller Inspectors, Assessor Developers, and Reporter Advisers.

In building an effective work team, it is important to share with your colleagues on a regular basis your thoughts and ideas. You may feel it inappropriate to talk through your theories until they are well thought out. However, unless your colleagues understand how your thinking is developing, they may feel left behind. Regular discussions can pay big dividends, even if they do take more time.

You probably feel you try to give your team a fair amount of autonomy. While you like to see things done your way, you want everyone to be themselves, so that their individual ways of doing things are respected. Overall, you can build an effective work team when you are able to delegate and trust others. This is, however, difficult when others do not understand or share your ideals, or let you down.

Your greatest strength is the innovative thinking and strong values you bring to the organization. Others may find it hard to understand these ideas. Your job is to help them appreciate what you see clearly and they can only dimly see. You may be hurt by what you perceive as criticism. Try not to take it personally. Treat criticism of your ideas as a problem statement to be discussed and resolved. You won't always be right and neither will your critics.

You will probably do well in a co-ordinating role, as long as people share your values. You will have an interest not only in advising others, but also in controlling the detail and direction. However, to ensure work gets finished on time, you will probably need others, particularly Concluder Producers, to complement your efforts.

Areas for self-assessment

Clearly, your approach has a number of strengths which can be extremely useful at work. However, one also needs to look at the other side of these strengths in order to develop a balanced profile. You may, therefore, find it useful to consider the following points.

You often do your best work when by yourself, rather than talking to others. Communication is, therefore, an important issue, unless you have developed good Linking skills. You will usually communicate well with a few tried and trusted people, but may perhaps be more reluctant to share your ideas with others at an early stage. If this is so, look at how you can improve communications, so that other people can understand your thinking as it develops, rather than having to absorb your innovative ideas in their full version. Your staff and colleagues need to be introduced to the complexity of your thinking in a series of on-going steps.

Ideas are your strength. Gathering detailed facts can be an area for development. If so, ensure that you have someone working with you who is strong on practical details and the provision of relevant information.

When it comes to substantial decisions, you should spend more time doing a detailed, objective analysis of the costs and benefits, rather than just relying on your ideas and beliefs. Again, it may be useful to have someone working with you who is a bit more detached and can look at some of these issues objectively.

Once you have developed an idea, your inclination will usually be to get on with the action. However, you will probably need the support of others to implement your proposals fully, given your own preferences for advisory work. A person with a Thruster Organizer profile can be very helpful in such situations.

Overall, you will bring to your job many strengths. In particular, you will play a key role in the team of maintaining relationships and standards, and upholding principles important to the organization and yourself. Alongside this, you will bring in new ideas and ways of tackling problems, and an ordered approach to dealing with difficulties.

Key points of note for Upholder Maintainers

- You are usually quietly confident and persevering in the team's interests.
- You tend to be strong on ideas and innovation.
- You may prefer a co-ordinating, advisory role, but will act in an executive role.
- You tend to be individualistic, and it is sometimes hard for others to know what you are thinking.
- Your personal convictions and beliefs are important in your decision-making.
- You are often single-minded and determined about ideas in which you believe.
- You may be easily hurt by criticism of your ideas or behaviour.
- You continually look for new approaches to old problems.
- You enjoy work where there is a wider meaning or purpose.
- You need to work with others who are strong on details regarding costs and benefits.
- You can concentrate for long periods working alone, although you like to balance this with time spent 'managing by wandering around'.
- You may support community organizations as a voluntary worker.
- You enjoy a close working relationship with a few trusted colleagues.

- Your enthusiasm and optimism can be great strengths.
- You have the ability to see opportunities and possibilities, often in advance of others.
- You can represent the organization effectively if you believe in the cause and are well briefed.
- You have the ability to communicate clearly and usually succinctly.
- You express yourself well in writing.
- You need regularly to review your priorities, to ensure they have not been subverted by other people's.
- You can take a lot of time to be supportive and helpful to others.
- You dislike sudden change and prefer gradual evolution.
- You appreciate specific recognition and appreciation for what you have done.
- You have a strong sense of what is 'right and wrong' and 'good and bad' and this guides your decision-making.
- You can uphold and maintain traditions and values in the organization.

Related roles

In the constructs of the Team Management Questionnaire, you scored strongest in the areas of creative information gathering and structured organization. These two factors have combined with your scores on the other two factors to locate you in the Upholder Maintainer sector of the Team Management Wheel. Here, you will want to work in a supportive way, advising others and ensuring that work is done to the high standards you usually expect. Your related roles lie in the sectors of Explorer Promoter and Thruster Organizer.

This pattern of scoring gives you an unusual pattern on the Team Management Wheel, where you have a three-way split, something that is observed in less than 1 per cent of people who have completed the Team Management Questionnaire. Basically, you can be quite creative, exploring how new ideas and opportunities can improve the work of your team. Where you are convinced that an idea will improve the efficiency of your particular part of the organization, you will often take that idea and push it into operation. At these times, you are more likely to be acting as a Thruster Organizer, but unlike people who have the Thruster Organizer sector as their major profile you are unlikely to ignore people's feelings, as these are paramount to the values by which you lead your life. Your style of Thruster Organizer behaviour will be more low-key, pushing things through on your own, as you will often believe the best way to get things done is to do them yourself, and not bother telling others until it is 'too late'.

Your preferences, to some extent, cover all four major parts of the Team Management Wheel – Exploring, Advising, Organizing, and Controlling – and you are likely to be able to adapt to most situations. In some circumstances, though, this split of the Wheel may make you cautious in implementing ideas that are your own. You will want to make sure things are 'just right' before proceeding, and at times this may cause you to get 'bogged down'.

While on balance you prefer to be quieter and more reflective, there are times when you can be more outgoing, particularly with people you know well or when you feel very sure of your facts. At these times, you are more likely to be wearing your Explorer Promoter 'hat'. Here, you will want to know about the latest ideas and technology that impact on your area of the organization. You will be quite receptive to new ideas and, where these coincide with your beliefs, you can become very persuasive and an advocate for their implementation.

You have an ability to organize people and events without too much preparation or planning. Often, you will rely on a 'sixth sense' to tell you what is right. This is a combination of insight, strong values and feelings, telling you what is appropriate and what is inappropriate. In general, you will be a good planner, for you like to know 'who' is doing 'what', to 'whom' and 'when'.

Overall, you are a tolerant person, and some may say not hard enough on people who deserve criticism. However, you will usually see the best in people and are often prepared to give them 'one more chance'. You will give loyalty but expect it in return and may, therefore, feel personally disappointed when people let you down.

Norm data

You may be interested to know how your scores match up against various reference groups. In the tables below, you will see how your scores compare with others in the indicated reference groups.

To interpret the data, examine each line in a table, paying particular attention to the percentages over 50. These will show how you compare with other people on each of the four work preference measures.

For example, in the first table, you will see that you prefer a more extroverted approach to work than 31.8 per cent of the database, and therefore a more introverted approach to work than 68.2 per cent of the database. A similar interpretation applies for the other work preference measures.

The profile descriptions given here relate to the information provided in the team management index. Whilst utmost care and attention has been taken, the authors and publishers stress that each profile is based on general observations, and they cannot be held responsible for any decisions arising from the use of the data, nor any specific inferences or interpretations arising therefrom.

Worldwide sample
Sample Size: 73,698

Extrovert	31.8%	Introvert	68.2%
Practical	23.2%	Creative	76.8%
Analytical	15.0%	Beliefs-orientated	85.0%
Structured	75.4%	Flexible	24.6%

Worldwide male sample
Sample Size: 41,682

Extrovert	32.4%	Introvert	67.6%
Practical	24.8%	Creative	75.2%
Analytical	12.0%	Beliefs-orientated	88.0%
Structured	74.6%	Flexible	25.4%

Worldwide female sample
Sample Size: 24,744

Extrovert	31.2%	Introvert	68.8%
Practical	20.1%	Creative	79.9%
Analytical	19.9%	Beliefs-orientated	80.1%
Structured	76.6%	Flexible	23.4%

Median score for selected reference groups
You may like to compare your own net Team Management Questionnaire scores with the median scores of the various nominated reference groups. Your net score is calculated by subtracting the raw scores for each work preference measure, as shown at the beginning of this profile. For each reference group, the median score indicates the point at which 50 per cent of people have a higher net score; therefore the remaining 50 per cent have a lower net score.

Group	Medians			
Your scores	I: 6	C: 8	B: 2	S: 10
Worldwide sample	E: 1	P: 1	A: 11	S: 4
Worldwide male sample	E: 1	P: 1	A: 12	S: 4
Worldwide female sample	E: 3	P: 3	A: 9	S: 3

An A–Z of Team Management Systems

A
Advising
> The work function of gathering and reporting information.

Analytical work preference
> A preferred way of making decisions by assessing facts impartially, rather than on specific beliefs or values.

Assessor Developer work preference
> A term to describe the behaviour pattern of a person who prefers to assess and test the applicability of new approaches.

Active listening
> Linking skill (people) ensuring that we listen well when others are addressing us. It helps to ensure that we understand the message, and the other person knows that we understand it.

B
Beliefs-work preference
> A preferred way of making decisions by judging the situation and evidence based on personal values and convictions, rather than detached analysis.

C
Creative work preference
> A preferred way of working that puts ideas and theories ahead of a practical pragmatic approach.

Creator Innovator
> A term to describe the behaviour pattern of a person who prefers to work in a way that generates ideas, theories and experiments to see if they work in practice.

Concluder Producer work preference
>   A term to describe the behaviour pattern of a person who prefers to
>   work in a systematic and regular way, to get tasks done according to
>   a plan and schedule.

Controller Inspector work preference
>   A term to describe the behaviour pattern of a person who prefers to
>   work in such a way as to control and audit work systems to ensure
>   compliance procedures are fulfilled.

D

Developing
>   The work function of assessing and testing applications and
>   new approaches.

Diagnosis
>   One of the key applications of the Team Wheel.

Delegation
>   The Team Wheel aids the process of deciding what to delegate.

E

Energy at work
>   The effort generated by individuals and teams when they have a
>   common team system with which to work.

External Linking
>   The links that are made between team members and those outside
>   the team, such as suppliers or clients, in order to establish closer
>   working relationships.

Explorers
>   Those who have a work preference for searching out new opportunities.

Extroverted work preference
>   A preference for working more with others, rather than in an
>   introverted way.

Explorer Promoter work preference
>   A term to describe a person who prefers to work in a way that looks
>   at new ways of doing things, and is keen to persuade others to adopt
>   these approaches.

F

Flexible work preference
>   A preferred way of working in which personal needs for doing things
>   in one's own time are put ahead of an external, scheduled, organized
>   and systematic approach to work.

Feedback
>Provided in a profile that enables you to read your work preferences based on your completion of the Team Management Questionnaire.

G
Goals
>The objectives, as defined by the team and team members based on the nine key areas of the Team Wheel.

H
High-energy teams model
>Research into high-performing teams identified eight key questions that a team should be able to answer collectively. This approach helps a group to chart its progress as it addresses these issues.

I
Innovating
>The work function of creating and experimenting with ideas.
Inspecting
>Controlling and auditing contracts and procedures.
Institute of Team Management Studies
>The organization that collects, assesses and manages the wealth of data on the TMS questionnaires in order to produce the annual report and review of trends.
Internal Linking
>The links that are made between one team member and another in order to establish closer working relationships.
Introverted work preference
>A preference for working more by oneself, rather than in an extroverted way.
Interface management
>Linking with others at work to ensure more effective action.

J
Jung, Carl
>The Swiss psychologist whose theories about personality types form the theoretical underpinning for the TMS work-preferences approach to understanding people at work.

K
Knowledge management
>This is enhanced by the application of TMS to business operations.

L

Linking

The skills of co-ordinating and integrating the work of others.

Linking Skills Profile Questionnaire

A measure which provides an opportunity for a person to gain feedback on how other people see their Linking skills.

Language of teamwork

The nine major factors in the Team Wheel form the basis for a common language to aid communication at work.

M

Maintaining

The work function of upholding and maintaining work standards and values.

Margerison and McCann

The authors of TMS (Dr Charles Margerison and Dr Dick McCann).

Multi-cultural

Through the on-going efforts of the Institute of Team Management Studies, culturally reliable foreign-language versions of the TMS questionnaires and reports have been developed. TMS is a common language used to transcend many cultural factors and issues.

N

Norm data

The research work provides comparative data for more than 100 reliable reference groups.

O

Organizing

The work function of organizing, establishing and implementing ways of making things work.

Objective-setting

A key aspect of Linking skills.

P

Producing

The work function of concluding and delivering outputs.

Promoting

The work function of exploring and presenting opportunities.

Practical work preference

A preferred way of working that puts pragmatic tools and techniques before theories and ideas.

Participative decision-making

A factor in Linking skills.

Problem-solving and counselling
    Another aspect of Linking skills.

Q

Questionnaire
    The Team Management Questionnaire, which is a reliable and fully-researched tool for assessing people's work preferences.
Quality standards
    A feature of Linking skills.

R

Research
    Research on TMS is conducted by the Institute of Team Management Studies, with its database of information derived from over 100,000 contributors.
Reporter Adviser work preference
    A term to describe the behaviour pattern of a person who prefers to take time to gather and understand information in depth before reporting, advising and taking action.

S

Structured work preference
    A preferred way of working that puts an organized and systematic approach ahead of a flexible personal-choice approach.

T

Team Management Systems (TMS)
    Brings together personal aspects, job requirements, team dynamics and Linking skills to get things done.
Types of Work
    The eight major work functions described in the Types of Work Wheel.
Thruster Organizer work preference
    A term to describe the behaviour pattern of a person who prefers to work in a way that organizes things and people to get tasks done according to a system and on time.
Team Management Profile Questionnaire
    A measure of people's team work preferences.
Team Performance Questionnaire
    A measure of how team members and others see the performance of a team.
Type of Work Questionnaire
    A measure of how a person sees his or her job on the eight major work functions, with the opportunity to compare it to the views of others.

Team relationships
> An important feature of Linking skills.

Team development
> A key activity in Linking skills.

U

Upholder Maintainer work preference
> A term to describe a person who prefers to work in a way that upholds valued ways of doing things based on beliefs, principles and traditions, as well as upholding standards and quality on tasks.

V

Values at work
> The system of cognitions and beliefs that are reflected in work preferences and job choices.

W

Wheels
> The two Team Wheels are: the Types of Work Wheel, referred to in this work as the Team Wheel describing the major work functions and tasks of a team; and the Team Management Wheel, describing the way different people prefer to work.

Work functions
> The eight major types of work that, together with Linking skills, constitute the core elements of any teamwork.

Work preferences
> A term that describes people's interests and preferred ways of working.

Work allocation
> A key Linking skill.

X

Xenophobia
> TMS can help minimize the effects of this condition of fear by enabling everyone to discuss their contribution and how it links and relates to others.

Y

Yourself
> The Team Wheel has been designed for individuals to understand and develop themselves at work.

Z

There is no specific term in the TMS lexicon based on the letter Z, so I invite you to add your own.

References

Books

The work in this book is based on research by Charles J. Margerison and Dick McCann inclusive of material described in:

TMS Research Manual, 2nd edition, TMS, Institute of Team Management Studies, Brisbane, 2001.

Team Management Systems: New Practical Approaches, Mercury 2000 Publications, 1995.

Team Re-engineering, TMS Australia Publications, 1995.

References to other publications

Harman, W., and H. Rheingold, *Higher-Creativity: Liberating the Unconscious for Breakthrough Insights*, J.P. Archer Inc., Los Angeles, 1984.

Jung, C., *Psychological Types*, Routledge, London, 1923.

Publication permissions

All figures are reproduced by the kind permissions of the publisher, Prado Systems Ltd.

All research statistics are reproduced by kind permission of the Institute of Team Management Studies, PO Box 1107, Milton, Brisbane, Queensland, Australia (e-mail: tms@tms.com.au; website: http://www.tms.com.au).

Website references

UK and Europe: http://www.tmsdi.com
North and South America: http://www.tms.com.au

Index

accountants 24, 31, 47, 59, 78, 160
acquisitions 56
action plans 62, 81, 101
active listening 70, 108, 109, 161
administration 59, 94, 115, 153
advertising 118
advertising agencies 53, 90–91
Advising work function 6, 8, 9, 22–24,
    54, 136, 143, 149, 151
  independent consultation 30–31
  information technology and 25–26
  linking assessment 20
  people with skills in 31, 124–125,
    126–127, 146, 147
  producing and 78
  projects 24–25
  research into 153–163
  team applications 15–16
  team linking 117–118
  team members' contribution 11
  two main areas of 27–28
  'view-to-do' meetings 26–27
Africa, Team Wheel research in 153,
    155–156
age work preferences 160–161
air-conditioning systems 97
airport check-in procedures 85
airworthiness 86
Amnesty International 102
Anson, John 99
architects 9, 114

Asia, Team Wheel research in 153,
    155–156
assembly lines 78
assessment 8, 162
Assessor Developers (work prefer-
    ence) 124, 128–129, 137, 140, 145
audits 90, 94, 120
Australia 7, 102, 152
Australasia, Team Wheel research in
    153, 155–156
aviation industry 86–87, 98, 100–101

Baker, Rob 15–16
banking industry 9, 14, 102, 156–157
  teams in 135–136
Barnes, Jane 142
Bayes, Susan 59
benchmark evaluation 71, 100, 119
Bennet, Wayne 35–37
Bhopal disaster 84
Blake, John 47
Body Shop 102
boundary-riding 113
brain-storming sessions 39
British Legion 102
budgets 24, 31, 54
bulletin boards 26
business development 57, 63
business information 22–33
  back-up of 92
business plans 57